SINGLE AND COMPLETE

BY

SEAN CORT

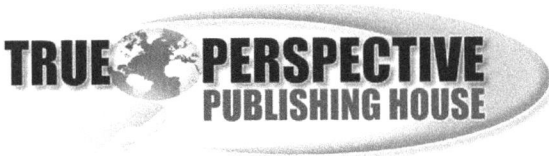

ACKNOWLEDGEMENTS

For my Lord and Savior Jesus Christ, I devote all I am and all I do to your glory for acceptance as my offering of thanksgiving and worship. Lord, in You alone do I live and breathe.

The Lord gave me a purpose and that is to inspire, encourage and heal the lives that cross my path. In this season of my life He has charged me with the fulfilling mission to empower women who don't get the encouragement and nurturing they deserve.

My sister and friend, my request to you is that you share what you get from this book with your fellow sisters throughout our human family. The Lord and the men in your life need you to be whole and complete.

Jazmin "Jazzy" Trespalacios and Janice Robinson. Thank you for giving me the platform to launch what the Lord gave me to do.

AUTOGRAPH PAGE

Make it personal by autographing this book to yourself or as a
gift to that special Single and Complete young lady

TABLE OF CONTENTS

INTRODUCTION

Both you and I have encountered women who frame their entire life around the existence or the preparation for the arrival of a man. This should come as no surprise considering that one of the top ten fears that women around the world say they contend with is that of growing old alone.

A woman will lose her friends, her family, her job, her credit, her money, her self-respect, her identity and eventually her soul for a man.My sister, this is an example of what can happen if you allow a man to try to occupy the role that only God should fill. God will never allow you to find fulfillment in any man unless you have sought true fulfillment and intimacy in Him first.

We are all spiritual beings, so the purpose of this book is to help you as a single woman to see the importance of getting your spiritual life, purpose and fulfillment in place first with God. If you are first complete as an individual then you will not desperately and unconsciously seek for anyone to complete you. Your realized purpose given to you from God will yield you more satisfaction than anything this life can offer you.

It does exist you know. My question is, since you show the world your outer strength; do you possess the inner courage to pursue the satisfaction that I'm speaking of? According to the U.S. Census 50% of U.S. marriages fail and over 75% of the single parent households are headed by women. There is enough pressure in the sheer odds in that statement to break most people. But you're still here. Don't you want more? Don't you think you deserve it?

This book will show you men from a whole new perspective. You will learn how to expand your horizons, break generational curses, while teaching you to pray, fight and scream while making you laugh, cry and deeply reflect. In the end you will make the most important change that this world will ever see, YOU

CHAPTER ONE

FOUNDATIONAL TRUTHS

The wonderful thing about footprints is that you can ignore them because they mean nothing. But if you chose to follow them they can mean everything.

DISCLAIMER

*W*hen you approach an amusement park attraction or open a package for a product that canbelethal or dangerous if the instructions are not followed accordingly, there is always a disclaimer or warning posted to help mitigate any liability from the manufacturer or service provider. Let's consider these words in that frame of mind for this book. I am not so concerned about mitigating liability as I am about being careful of setting your expectations. This is not the book for the slight of heart or those who have taken permanent domicile on the island of PC (politically Correct).

Although this book is not profane in the least or intended on being offensive, there are those who have an aversion to truth who may find this installment of The Power of Perspective book series as a bit strong. Please accept my apologies in advance if this individual is you. My purpose in life and God's intent for giving me The Power of Perspective brand, books and teaching series is never to offend but always to uplift and enhance one's perspective of their immediate surroundings and their purpose in at any given time in life. Always remember ***TRUTH merits no reward nor does it dignify a response. Like God, Truth is absolute and therefore supreme.***

Every single person that is of adult age needs to see this time in life as an opportunity to get better acquainted with their inner self mentally and spiritually. Being a single as a young adult should be viewed as a toddler views the many moving parts of their ever increasing daily universe. From the perspective of an adult, a toddler spends painstaking hours examining their toes, their fingers and the other body parts that strike their curiosity. To that child there is nothing painstaking about this time at all.

This child is taking an assessment of all that belongs to them and how these appendages are used and how they can be of service once their legs get them to another curious place in their universe. As a young single adult you should be doing the same things as this child is doing; only now you have a bit more experience and knowledge on how to apply this curiosity. At this point in your live you now know the questions to ask. You may even be blessed with the wisdom of knowing what to ask.

The glorious world of being single can bring about all kinds of emotions for the single person depending on the circumstances that got them there. Regardless of what circumstances got you to the point of single-dom, you should always make sure that you take the opportunity to assess your world physically, mentally and spiritually.

You may be single now because of a recent breakup with your boyfriend. Maybe he cheated on you, maybe you cheated on him. Perhaps like the 75 plus million adults in this country, you are divorced. An interesting fact is according to the 2000 U.S. Census, 93% of the divorces in this country are initiated by the woman. So be informed that if you are in this number that you are not broken, or dysfunctional. I am divorced twice and I initiated them both. So I am not on a pulpit preaching down to you in the back pew. I'll share my story with you during the pages of this book as well.

You may be a widow who is trying to get balance back into her life. Or maybe you have never been married, simply because you haven't been asked or it didn't feel right. Whatever your situation, I promise you by the time you put this book down that you will have learned something new in a way that you haven't had it told to you. If you have heard it, you will find that this is now that season and this is how you were to understand and apply it to your life. Every harvest has its season.

An apple seed doesn't become an apple orchard in three months. Read these stories with an open mind and be willing to accept that in order to get what you want that you may need to change a few things. Not because he told you so, but because He told you so. God is absolute and He has and will always have the final word.

There is nothing in this book that is new under the sun. But if a revolution is what you want in your life then you must understand two things. Any revolution is birthed from desperation and timing. You must want the change so bad that you are willing to forego pride and concern for the opinion of others. The timing must be right or you will exert the right energy but at the wrong time. If a man is attacking you, you are already desperate to get out of the situation.

You must wait to exert your desperate thrust for freedom at his weakest spot when it is posed to you not when it is protected.

The changes you want in your life are actively seeking you as well. It is God's promise to you in (John 10:10) *Ihave come that they may have life, and have it to the full*.

Jesus does not desire that anything be withheld from you except that which is bad for you. We all may have wanted a nice shiny red sports car for our 18th birthday. But many of us would not still be alive today because we would have gotten ourselves killed or carjacked if we did get what we want. So don't think for a second that you are not loved by the Lord with Him allowing certain aspects of life to be withheld from you now.

Like the curious toddler mentioned a few paragraphs above it is very important that we never lose that transparent interest in the assets that are hidden in plain sight in our lives. As we get older we tend to allow our sophistication and our experiences to dull our senses and sensibility to take note of all the wonder and merriment that use to bring us hours of enjoyment as a child.

One may say that we are no longer children and should put away childish things. I certainly agree. But there is something to be said about winning wars and slaying giants and still being able to be relevant to a toddler. Pablo Ruiz Picasso is universally renowned as a painter, sculptor and co-founder of the cubist movement in the art world. He literally thought and created outside of the box. Picasso said, "Every child is an artist. The problem is how to remain an artist once we grow up."

This master artist and thinker nailed the dilemma of becoming a tainted adult. Once life teaches us, beats us up and betrays us a bit; as result we tend to lose our innocence and transparency forever.

You may have become single from a variety of reasons and in this term that society has labeled you, there may be children and others that you are responsible for. So in actuality you may not be single at all, just without someone you want to be with who can help you grow, heal and carry the load. Here is where foundational truths are important. Being single doesn't mean that you must also be single-minded. Being single presents you with the opportunity to begin again on your own terms but with clarity and truth.

Many stop at the part where I said, "on your own terms." What's the point if you only see things your way and that way is the wrong way? This will mean that you will continue to keep failing forward and pulling your loved ones and those destined in your path along with you. If you said ouch here, you are not alone. Even if you are only able to say "ouch" when you are alone, then this is a good thing, there are some of us, who cannot even say ouch at all.

This is because there are no nerve endings where there was once immense pain. So in order to curtail the constant attack, the nerve had to be removed or bypassed.

Let's see if we can bring back the sensation in that spot. Not so you can hurt again but so you can have blood flow and feel again. Being able to say ouch is a very good thing. Once someone is rushed to the emergency department or a trauma unit of a hospital one of the first things they asses is the patient's ability to have feeling or sensation in the part of the body that received the trauma. Feeling pain becomes a very good thing, feeling no pain is a sign of serious damage.

When you are an adult who has been through some stuff and you have survived despite life and its cruelty, then you tend to feel a bit self-righteous for still being here. The important thing to remember is that you are still here despite yourself not despite life.

If we had the power to leap forward 50, 60 or 70 years and look back over our life. How much of what you stood up for or stuck your neck out for, would still be worth it? Quite naturally defending your peace of mind, your faith and your children will always be worth it.

But how many times was your pride, your ego or your status worth the ensuing stormy seasons that you brought on yourself? Chances are, not much. That's why our beloved seniors tend to not get bent out of shape about people and what they think anymore. They already know the punch line to the joke. The punch line is, most people are just older kids who pretend better than toddlers.

To help set the stage I'll share an excerpt from a weekly E-devotional I write called Snack Food for the Soul. It's called:

THE INTRICACY OF A WOMAN

A woman's role has evolved immensely. Today the delicate balance must be struck between being a woman, behaving like a lady and too often, having to think like a man. Most women have to struggle with their greatest adversary daily, their mind. She must brave the winds of insecurity and competitiveness almost daily. In her academic and vocational environment if she is too aggressive, smart or competent she must grapple with the forged labels of bossy or other non-flattering words. If she displays superior intellectual, mental or athletic prowess her femininity is questioned.

The mere mention of the title denotes a wordy and involved dissertation. The fact is depending on what continent you live, the intricacy of a woman's psyche is based on one word, security. This is not to minimize in the least the extreme complexities that constitute a woman's physiological makeup. After all, these magnificent specimens are engineered to be the cradle of life's inception.

If you are looking to invest in one of the world's most exclusive diamonds such as a 4K Princess Ideal-Ideal cut you would have to make appropriate accommodations for its security. This is not the kind of acquisition you store in your velvet lined jewelry box purchased from Target. The same forethought was employed by God when He made His investment in Eve.

All the elements of creation had its name and were in place to accommodate her arrival. Her primary need for security was satisfied by the provision of covering from all the elements by man under the shadow of the almighty. Woman was not created to provide, she was created to be provided for. The nostrils of a woman are constantly tortured by the recurring stench of double standards that plague her world.

A woman always has to exceed all the highest expectations just to be considered man's contender. The turbines of her mind must always turn just to stay ahead of man's incessant game of stares, jeers and his wares. This lends itself to her desperate need for authenticity.

A woman has to pretend so much that it hurts my head just to think about it. It is so obvious when a man has not yet reached manhood but so difficult for a woman to come to terms with her inability to manage her womanhood. A woman has a dense and intricate design so therefore it is easier to hide her flaws.

Here's the double standard; the transmission flaws of a diesel engine in a tractor trailer are easier to hide than the precision tuned engine of a Bugatti Veyron. That diesel engine can just tug and jerk and it's called character but the moment a CD skips in the Bugatti's stereo it's time to have it checked out. Sound familiar?

So who helps a woman to manage her womanhood like a lady when she is fed up with life treating her like she's a little girl? There is a Jewish carpenter born without an earthly father who grew up in a blended family by the name of Jesus. He said in Matthew 11:28 "Come unto me all you who are weary and heavy laden and I will give you rest".

Jesus wants to give you peace and a change of heart. He wants you to come to Him as naked and transparent as you came into this world. It was never His desire for you to carry the burdens you have.

Even though life and its people have let you down, He is not mankind He is God. He wants to provide for you the same way He provided for Eve. Even though you may not have had the best parental covering as a child; Jesus loves you enough to mentor you Himself. Will you let Him?

Dare to ask Him to change your eyeglass prescription to His perspective, so that you can now see everything and everyone through His eyes. You will soon find that life no longer beats on you, but your heart beating in unison with His. You are an Ideal-Ideal precious specimen of God.

HOW SPECIAL YOU ARE TO GOD

There were some great men placed in my life by God, but they were few and didn't last too long. The women I became close with as mentors or friends didn't have too many male role models in their life either so we had lots of gaps to fill together. The fact that I'm writing this book should not negate the importance of a strong man with Christian values in the life of anyone, but reality is, there just aren't enough of them to go around. If you happen to know a man who is holding up his end of the bargain make sure you encourage him to continue the course and to positively affect as many lives as he can.

As a young man all I kept hearing from those around me was making sure that one day you can take care of your wife and her protector and her covering. You as a woman are so special to God that He made sure all things were in place before

He created you. His intention was for you to be the co-executor of His garden. Most people feel that Eve was created to serve Adam. Not at all. Eve was created equal to Adam in every way. The subservient and competitive role was assigned after the first sin in the Garden. God created the woman as the cradle of life and with the inherent ability to nurture, critically think and to multi-task.

Down through the years man has gotten it all wrong as to how the woman should be treated. It was God Himself that would call out certain women in the bible's Old Testament to come forward and change history. Later on as Jesus came forward he proved Himself to be the first civil rights leader. On the cross when he said, "It is Finished", he tore the veil in two allowing Jew or Gentile, saint or sinner and even women as well as men to gain free access to the throne God. Jesus had at least 11 women who traveled with Him on a regular basis. They were:

- *Mary, the mother of Jesus*
- *Mary Woman with an issue of blood—Matthew 10:20*

- *the mother of James and Joses—Matthew 27:55–56*
- *Mary Magdalene—Luke 8:2–3, Mark 15:40, Matthew 27:56, John 19:25, and Luke 23:49*
- *Mother of Zebedee's sons—Matthew 27:55–56*
- *Priscilla—Romans 16:3*
- *Salome—Mark 16:1*
- *Sisters Mary and Martha—Luke 10:38, John 11:1–44*
- *Tabitha/Dorcas—Acts 9:36*
- *Widow of Nain—Luke 7:11–17*
- *Woman bent double—Luke 13:10–17*

These are women who kept the men together when the socially unacceptable men that Jesus chose would get out of line. One of the many things I love about Jesus is that he chose people that were a little rough around the edges because he knew they had the greatest bandwidth for growth. Think about it; fishermen were not the cream of the crop in terms of their etiquette training and social graces. In fact His disciples had personalities that greatly varied from each other. Social scientists today say there are about four different personality types that are sub divided down to another four in each category.

It is believed that Jesus chose a man to represent each of them. How else would he be able to minster to us and understand how we would one day be unless He had to contend with each on a personal level? Every major move of God involved a woman a woman who stood close by.

Back in the garden when God cursed Eve with suffering and pain during child delivery He gave her the very thing that she would need to be able to reach God during her most trying time. This gift was the gift of travailing. Women can travail where as men can't. Men don't know anything about travailing. We can scream and moan but nothing compares to a woman who can grab her belly in a slumped over position as though she is about to deliver. God gave the woman the urge to compete with man and that urge can be the cause of a lot of heartache. This further creates pride and arrogance between the sexes. The ability to travail puts your prayer life into hyper-drive. This means that you have the ability to reach the presence of God faster than most men just by virtue of the fact that you can cry out to the Lord and reach His heart from your broken state.

Men have to push past our ego, bravado, selfishness and immaturity just to get into the spirit. By the time we feel a touch of His glory, the woman got there and left already with her deliverance. In the next few chapters we will delve into some things that you may already know but haven't heard in a while.

THE TOWER OF BABEL

Let's face it as a result of Eden men and women will never speak the same language. We process the same things differently and as a result our needs in the same situations will be different. That is probably the cause for why we have all been single at some point in our lives. The purpose of this book is to help you see the importance of getting your life and personal purpose and fulfillment in place first. If you are first complete then you will not be looking for anyone to complete you. You will see that seeking and finding God's purpose for you in your service to Him will be the most gratifying aspect of life.

God said in (Exodus 20:3) *"You shall have no other gods before me."* God is so serious about this statement that He made it a commandment. I know scores of women who go through life and pattern their existence about finding a man. One of the biggest fears women have today is being alone.

A woman will lose her friends, her family, her job, her credit, her money, her self-respect, her identity and eventually her soul for a man. I've seen it happen. My sister, this is an example of having a god in place of God. God will never allow you to find fulfillment in any man unless you have sought true fulfillment in Him first.

Any man that is willing to become your god in a relationship is a false idol and you become the idolater, which simply means idol worshipper. Both you and I know women like this. They will do anything for their man but they can't remember the last time they gave a fraction of that devotion to God. They neglect their children and their welfare and not to mention the covering of their children just to keep the biggest baby in their life happy.

 A man is not given to you to take care of like a child; a man is given to you to cover you, support you, promote you and challenge you to become the biggest and best example of Christ in your home and your community that God will allow.Any man that is intimidated by your beauty, intelligence, natural glow and charm is intimidated by God's anointing on your life. In time God will allow this man and his carnally driven insanity to destroy all you have built because your foundation was not built on Christ the solid rock; so it will fall to the ground in sinking sand. I am not wishing this terror on anybody because it is true terror.

I am merely saying that God is a jealous God and He will have no other God exalted above Him in the earth, the galaxy and any other form of creation. If you have recently gotten out of such a relationship; right this moment you should raise your hand and say "Thank you Jesus for rescuing me." I have seen and heard women lose their lives in sin and their children too because of the dreaded fear of not being without a man or the man who use manipulation and witch craft upon her weakened state to have her think that she needs him.

I have two English Mastiff dogs as pets. Their names are Kenya and Winston. In my eyes they are the most beautiful dogs God has ever created. They are both over 200 lbs. and are as sweet and gentle as can be. There are times that I just let them sit in the front yard to watch people go by. The neighbor that is immediately across the street from me is a piano teacher and the dogs are accustomed to sitting or lying there like statues and watching the cars pull up and kids going in and out of the house.

My office looks out at them so I can watch them as I work. The families that drop off the kids look forward to seeing these behemoths sitting pretty like their championship bloodlines should dictate.

They don't bark nor do they chase anyone. They know their place because of their instinct to guard what is their own. Every now and then one of the children will come over to pet Winston. Since he is the goofy one of the two dogs he may get up and greet the visitor without looking at me for permission. When I know he is in enough of a playful mood I would chain him to keep him from jumping into someone's car and giving them a heart attack. One end of the chain would be clipped to his collar and the other half would be hooked to a twig on a flower bush or some small plant.

So as soon as he feels the slightest resistance he would stop immediately and go back to sit down. *He doesn't know that he could probably uproot a small tree if he truly wanted to, but he knows that tension on the chain indicates an extension of my authority*. He will never challenge that authority because he knows he will get yelled at and he hates to be yelled at. When he gets yelled at he won't eat and he cowers in the corner. That is the nature of English Mastiffs; they are very sensitive and want nothing more than to please their owner.

27

This is the same premise they train circus elephants on. As the elephant is a baby they tie him to a stake that he cannot pull out. As he gets older and heavier he is conditioned to respect the authority of the chain. When he is fully grown he could probably uproot a fully grown oak tree or a house off its foundation. The trick is when he is older they simply use a small stake in the ground to keep the elephant in one spot. The elephant's mind still thinks the stake is too strong for his might so he obeys and remains. *He is never told of his full potential otherwise he would not be able to be controlled.*

This is the same tactic that school bullies and insecure husbands use on their wives that they are intimidated by. They feel the need to first break her down and separate her from her support system and her self-confidence and respect. This may take time but like satan, he is patient.

He knows the treasure he has in you. Just like satan knows the treasure that you are to Christ. If he could not sense your value in the Lord, he would leave you alone like a penny with a hole in it.

These weak men use the same mental ball and chain that is used to train animals. She is never told that she can walk away from an abusive situation so she stays there obediently and frightfully in check. Just like my dogs they want you to cower and fear displeasing them.

I am here to tell you that you will never allow that to happen to you or anyone woman you know ever again. The devil is a liar and he is a dead man walking. The fact is no one has pronounced him dead yet. Of course not all men are like the monster I just described but satan is. So if you are not imprisoned by one you are likely to be imprisoned by the other if you are not complete in Christ first. If you swap your identity for the mind and spirit of Christ you will never lose yourself in a man again. This book will show you how wonderful life can be when you marry the King before you find your prince.

Before we begin, let's take care of first things first. You don't have to do this now, but I suggest you do it soon if you have not. I am speaking of the prayer of salvation. If you have tried everything else and you are not sure if you are truly saved and filled with the Spirit of Christ. Why don't we make sure right now.

This is between you and the Lord. No one even has to know what you are saying under your breath. Many folks don't say this prayer because they feel it has to take place in front of a bunch of strangers in a church. We can do this together right now.

"Father God, in the name of Jesus, I thank you for being God and preserving my life for this opportunity to acknowledge you as the only wise and true God of creation. I believe that you sent your only son Jesus Christ to suffer and die on the cross as your lamb of sacrifice for my sins so that I may have a chance to accept Him as my Lord and Savior, and have the right to eternal life with you in heaven.

Father, I ask that you please forgive me for all my sins of the past and present. Father, please wash me in the blood of Jesus and remove my sins and my desire to sin against you. Father, please forgive me for the words and deeds that I have spoken and committed against you and the body of Christ. Lord Jesus, please come into my heart and fill me with your precious Holy Spirit to guide, heal and protect me.

Father, please take away my taste and desire for sin. Please replace these sinly desires with a desire to please you and to pursue good Godly character and integrity. Father, please take away these urges I have to selfishly appease my flesh and replace these urges for a hunger and thirst after your righteousness.

Please give me the faith and courage to tell others about your love for them and your grace and mercy. By my profession of faith, Father, I declare that I am saved by your grace. Thank you Father, thank you Father, In Jesus name. Amen.

There is a wonderful life that God has prepared for you in this season. Let the Holy Spirit and *Single and Complete* be your travel partner as you journey down this exciting path; this time we'll follow the Lord's foot prints.

CHAPTER TWO

THE CHARACTERISTICS OF YOUR SEASON

Everything occurs in a season. If you know what season in your life you are currently in, then you will know where you are and why.

SEASONS AND CLIMATES

*E*cclesiastes 3:15 says, "There is an appointed time for everything. And there is a time for every event under heaven-- A time to give birth and a time to die; A time to plant and a time to uproot what is planted. A time to kill and a time to heal; A time to tear down and a time to build up. A time to weep and a time to laugh; A time to mourn and a time to dance. A time to throw stones and a time to gather stones; A time to embrace and a time to shun embracing…"

One of the things I miss about living in New York is the clear demarcation of the four seasons. You clearly had a chance to enjoy the slow transition from fall to winter and spring to summer. Having four seasons as opposed to one or two gives you the opportunity to miss one and prepare for the other. Although living on a private Island in the Caribbean or South Pacific does have pronounced merit, there is nothing more refreshing than a cool blast of cool air after a season of sweltering heat. Unless it is your preference, your life as someone who is not in a committed relationship should be viewed as your weather or your season but certainly not your climate.

Weather is a current state of atmospheric elements that may dictate conditions that are wet, dry, hot, cold, cloudy or clear. Depending on how drastic these elements are in our atmosphere, these conditions can change in a matter of hours or even minutes. Seasons are a bit more predictable and stable. You can predict seasonal changes in the weather almost to the day and you can determine how long they will stay.

Seasonal changes act as a slow transition between more extreme and prolonged weather conditions. A season changes every few months but a climate tends to be a yearlong occurrence. Take for instance the Caribbean, the South Pacific and the Arctic Circle. These regions of the world are well known for their consistent climate of either warm or cold.

A climate is determined by consistent and prolonged measurements of weather conditions over a period of years. This is why I often say that your weather or your season doesn't have to be your climate. Simply put, unless being single is your choice, your condition doesn't have to be your outcome. Within seasons various aspects of nature automatically rest, restore, die, grow or bloom. During this season of your life, make an assessment of what needs to occur in your life personally.

REST

This is a time when should take a moment and ask yourself; "how much sleep do I get on a daily basis?" Rest is a vital part of a bodies function. There is no way that you can refresh your body and mind if it has no time to reboot and refresh. I know that sounds easier said than done, but just because you have a busy lifestyle and get minimal sleep doesn't make it right.

Lack of sleep will age you and become the underlying reason for weigh gain, increased depression, memory loss, increased car accidents, heart disease, diabetes and put you at risk for a plethora of other physical and mental health challenges.

A healthy grown up can get by with 7 to 8 hours of uninterrupted sleep to function optimally each day. If you are not within that range and you are already experiencing one or more of the challenges mentioned, you are doing yourself a great dis-service. This is not meant to make a bad situation even worse. This is intended to help you successfully navigate through this season.

Whether you think you have all the answers or not, my prayer and determination is to see you through this season triumphantly. One of the many ways of carving time out of your bus day for more rest is by turning off the TV and opening a book.

Reading a book or periodical for leisure stimulates the brain in ways that a television show cannot. The brain actually receives more positive stimulation from sleep than it does watching TV. According to a 2009 study by the Nielsen Corporation, the average American spends approximately 153 hours a month watching TV.

That totals out to over 6 days out of a 30-day month watching TV. If you are an individual who gets minimal sleep because you spend precious hours winding down in front of the tube, you may want to rethink your relaxation time.

There are numerous ways to unwind besides TV. More importantly if you have access to the internet there are a thousand and one resources at your fingertips to aid your search for alternate ways of unwinding faster so you can hit the sack sooner. If you don't have a computer and you have multiple jobs then you need to view your health as the primary objective in your daily routine.

As a former single dad I thoroughly understand the need for getting out there and earning the cash to keep the household afloat. But bear in mind that killing yourself makes that notion an impossibility. The best insurance policy for your household is you being alive. If you are a single parent, few things take the place of giving your child a warm and unconditional smile or reassuring hug. An insurance check can't do that.

If you are a single person without the obligations of single parenthood then use this period of rest to remain healthy. Treat your health as a bank account with high yields and no risk. You may need to fully rely on those reserves one day.

DIE

Dying is never a word that brings about positive thoughts. However in this application the word dying is a very good thing. **Death is simply something making an exit so that something else can make an entrance.** During seasonal changes it is necessary for certain aspects of an organism in nature to die in order for the overall organism to flourish. Take for instance our skin; we need to exfoliate dead skin cells in order for fresh healthy skin cells to show forth. There are certain aspects of our character that need to slough off so that we can benefit from growth.

We all like to think that we are a work in progress and that we will eventually get there. But getting there in a timely manner is essential to being in season. Finding the love of your life and beginning the courting process is not the time to drop the baggage from your last three relationships.

The scar tissue you developed from the hurt and resentment of these bad experiences should have been dealt with and

34

reconciled in your spirit long before Prince Charming shows up in your life. It's un fair for him and unconscionable for you to unload all of your trash in the middle of a beautiful garden; your new relationship filled with potential. This season in your singleness should be a time for these hurts, coping mechanisms and flaws to be done away with.

This is what is referred to as death to self. During this time you as a vessel of God should seek to extinguish all the attributes of your life that separate you from getting to know and serve your God intimately. This action of love for the service of our God can be sought out easily but not easily demonstrated. Simply put, I can explain how to do it but you may find it difficult to accomplish. To distinguish the character traits that only serve you versus the character traits that serve God, examine these factors:

1. Are you overly sensitive or defensive when it comes to receiving constructive criticism?
2. When someone critiques your actions or your ideologies even with the kindest of words; do you instantly retort with a battery of excuses and explanations as if under cross examination? Do you find it difficult to simply receive it as an instructional moment that you can build on instead of trying to bury it?
3. Is the reason of all your break-ups due to a lack of effort on your partner's behalf and their inability to understand your thought process?
4. Do you spend more time talking on the phone and visiting social networking sites than patiently and consistently seeking God for His guidance and wisdom concerning the key areas of your life such as employment, social and relational issues with people and how to plan your waking moments serving Him?

5. How much time do you spend in the course of a week consulting the Holy Spirit on matters concerning your diet, choice of clothing and the words you choose in answer to certain questions and situations?
6. Are there people in your life that you resent and are holding forgiveness of them hostage until they do what you feel they should do to make things better?
7. Do you read the bible for yourself in order to get to know God, or do you rely on the preached word to process it for you?

If you have answered these questions honestly, then you have a true sense of how much of you is in service to the Lord and how much of you is in the way of the Lord. Certainly there are more questions that one can ask to derive the same conclusions. The point here is not to judge or to make one feel guilty. The objective is to help you see that the blessings and storms we experience are a direct result of what we have sewn spiritually and naturally.

There are certain instances where God reserves the right to just be God by allowing storms to come our way to simply test our faithfulness, help us mature or to get His glory. Other than that it is important to see that the laws of attraction are always in play in our lives. Whatever you sow you will reap. If you sow negativity then negativity will find its way to you. If you are the type of person that finds it easier to seek, think and speak negatively then these type of spirits will always cross your path and cause you heart ache.

The important thing to do is to ask yourself if you are this type of person. Your mind style is a major contributor to your lifestyle. You've heard the bible scripture that says, "so does a man thinketh, so is he." Your life will literally become what you think on a regular basis. There is an axiom I try to quote whenever I get the opportunity to: *"watch your thought for they become your words; watch your words for they become your actions; watch your actions for they become your habit; watch your habits for they become your character; watch your character for it becomes your destiny."*

It's always easier to blame the negatives in your life on someone or a random circumstance. It's seldom easy to be transparent before God or an accountability partner and simply admit that it's been your fault all along; and unless you change you will continue to shipwreck your life and every life you touch romantically.

Quite frankly you deserve better than that and so do the lives you touch. You know that wonderful feeling that consumes your world when you become smitten with love and the mere thought of that someone special completely consumes you.

That new feeling of love will make you smile more often, become positive in your outlook, take better care of yourself and even treat your co-workers and family members better. Love will make you clean your work space, clean your house, do your nails and change your packaging. Now imagine doing these things just because you feel that way about you. I'm not saying become more vain; but just imagine learning to appreciate you more. *My friend, it is actually possible to ask God to remove the dark and negative areas in your life and replace them with new life, new growth and sweet smelling flowers.*

In my book Bruised Yet Priceless, there is a chapter called Me Time that fully explains how to use your alone time to court yourself and fill in all the empty spaces that a relationship is no longer consuming. Allow empty spaces and lethargy to die also. By filling in these spaces with a greater band width of self-discovery and personal growth, you offer a broader dimension to those around you.

This dimension will even become more obvious to strangers. You've heard the saying that it's easier to find a date when you're not looking for one?Diminishing the appearance of desperatism or lack of depth makes any woman more appealing to a man.

Men like women with mystique. If that word sounds too spooky to you; men like women who are not flat and thin. Men like women who offer depth and texture. It's bad enough that many men think women are too predictable and miserable anyway. Let's not let the bad press of some women create prejudicial thinking for your life. Allow negative thinking, lethargy and indifference to die. During this season of your single-dom try to focus on the things about your character and thought process that bring no value spiritually and naturally to your life.

If they bring no value to you other than distraction and a meaningless addiction, then they will be s stumbling block to your personal development and future relationships.
The key to simply killing these useless areas off is by understanding the components of fear and how to dismantle it. We'll cover fear shortly.

RESTORE

After the natural destruction of something this is the part of the healing process where what was taken away is replenished. When beautiful summer lawns turn brown and almost completely dissipate, the warm sun and heavy rains help waken their ability to produce chlorophyll once again and turn our communities green.

The same is true for leaves, flowers and your life. After your break-up or whatever reason your single-dom exists, it's time to bring back the true beauty of you. When any possession is exposed long term to the elements it tends to lose its brilliance and natural appeal.

This is when the owner sloughs off the wear and tear and applies a layer of two of some fresh paint to restore it back to what it was originally.. This is when you reach deep within and bring back the vigor and drive that brought you so much happiness before struggle and strife were a notion. After the flood God replenished the earth; after Job's trial He restored all he had and even more. Even after a destructive forest fire, nature shows its innate ability to restore by faint signs of green boring their way through the black ash.

Part of the restoration in your life is allowing the joy that motivated you in your younger years to return. I'm not saying that you need to skip through life with an innocent and eternal grin on your face. That would be impractical and even silly. Restoration here says to see past the filters and prejudice that experience has weighed us down with.

Not all experience and sophistication has served us properly. Think of the number of times when your pre-disposition to draw rash conclusions has proven you wrong or even embarrassed you.

Think of the last wedding you may have attended where the bride and groom were young and totally in love. Was there a part of you that looked at them with pity and skepticism because of the rude awakening that love has brought you? When you hear of the familiar lullaby of new love being sung from the lips of a young person, do you cringe somewhere inside as if to say, "give it time, you'll see."

This is exactly the prejudice that I'm speaking of. Let's face it, you and I both have made our mistakes and have been the brunt of mistakes made against us. But that is just the problem. They were mistakes and in many cases painful ones. Just because you received sun burn from not taking the proper precautions doesn't mean that you should scorn a sun set or sunrise. When we begin to see all that is beautiful through eyes of skepticism then we are literally walking through life with one foot in the grave. *When one sees more negative than positive in the elements that bind us together, then life has long since left their soul; the issue is that no one has yet should them the compassion of pronouncing them dead.*

During this season of restoration try to remember what it was like to dream before anyone told you no, or before life's detours hijacked your dreams from you. Here are some simple thoughts and suggestions that may help soften your soul:

1. The next time you are in a shopping mall, try to find a seat where you can observe families walking who really seem to be enjoying their day. Pay particular attention to the children or their parents and see if your eyes can meet their eyes and smile. If they smile back try and remember when you have done the same as a child. Perhaps there is a little bit of fate returning the favor to you.

2. Buy lunch for a homeless person. It doesn't have to be a homeless person. It can be the person who you see can obviously use a blessing of that nature. Don't make it complicated, just express a random act of kindness in

40

due season. On your way out a restaurant slip a $5 bill in the hand of the bus boy and thank him for a great smile. Maybe the waitress three tables away looked like she could really use a reason to smile. In that case slip her a $10 bill. You would have just paid $15 to change two people's state of mind. Like the commercial states, there was a monetary value on your actions, but the repercussions are priceless..

3. Another real easy way to softening your heart is by walking into a hospital or hospice and asking if you can go and visit some patients. In the advent of patient privacy regulations, this may be more challenging to do than the previous two. But there is something to be said about being sick or dying in a room and a perfect stranger walks in to just share a smile and some good cheer. This is of special significance if the person has no one who visits them regularly. This will make them feel as though God truly loves them and help you to put your life in a perspective of gratitude.

Part of realizing the value of restoration is learning to not take yourself or your circumstances too seriously. God can change things for the better in the snap of a finger or allow things for the worse in the blink of an eye. In either case remember (1 Thessalonians 5:18 KJV) In everything give thanks: for this is the will of God in Christ Jesus concerning you." Paul said "In" everything give thanks not "For" everything give thanks. Regardless of which side of the blessing line or the skeptic line you are currently living on, remember that God can turn your situation around quicker than you can say "thank you Jesus."

GROWTH

The word grow is the cornerstone of Christian and personal development. Otherwise how can you claim anything unless you are able to live it? *You can only claim to be a part of something if you are willing to be apart from something else.* You must shed the old in order to grow the new. Grow is a verb thus indicating that it requires definitive and undisputable action. When you rest and allow aspects of your old mind set to die off, restoration takes place. Quite naturally during the restorative process growth takes place. This occurs when you decide to get over the separation anxiety that is caused by the habits you gave up.

Some times that habit includes resentment, pride, arrogance and denial. You would be surprised how many forms these characteristics can take on. For example consider the thin line between humility and arrogance. You may be the type of person who always sacrifices for others and always finds yourself doing the favor but never being favored by those you help.

It may be one dark and dreary day when life catches you off guard and someone you've helped in the past decides to say something to you like, "You are just like the rest, all you do is take, take, take." At that moment the thin line between humility and arrogance disappears as though it were never there.

You quickly find yourself retorting with phrases like, "after all I've done for you", or, "whenever someone comes to me for help I am there. In fact more people owe me than I can count. I of all people should never be called selfish." Do you see how the selfless intent of your actions are so easily eradicated by your words. This now begs the question of the initial motive behind those kind acts to begin with. Was the motive to be a blessing or was it to have the higher hand?

This is just one example of growth. You must be able to have an honest discussion with yourself about what you are willing to give up for your detriment and what you are willing to take on for your overall good.

Accepting that you are a 'Drama Queen' and that three quarters of your own misery is caused by you, takes a mature person. Now that you have faced this hypothetical fact, what are you willing to do to grow past this issue? Part of your answer should include accepting people as they are and loving them where they are without waiting 'til they leave the room to giggle and talk about them

Another solution to this hypothetical fact is to spend more time talking with the Spirit of God concerning keeping your mind and mouth under control. Your mind and your mouth can get you into a whole bunch of trouble. By understanding that people are essentially the same child but with different coping mechanisms, should be good enough reason to stop judging and start tolerating. If we all have the same father in God, then we should stop with the sibling rivalry. After all, If God is your father too and all he sees is you posturing yourself above your other siblings then you have actually elevated yourself to the problem child. God is not a respecter of persons.

God is not impressed with what you know, what you've achieved or what you've been told. God is not impressed with the weight you've lost, the way you look and your apparent lack of mistakes. God is only impressed with how you make Him feel during the most trying and traumatic times of your life.

If you make Him feel like Lord and King in your life by the way you treat the "least of these" (Matthew 25:31-46) and He is also treated as King and Lord of your life when you are on the mountain top or valley, then you have the makings of something to talk about. This is the classic example of growth.

43

BLOOM

This means exactly as it reads. This is where you shine after all you've been through. By the lushness of your bloom one can tell the depth of your roots. The more strong your root system is the more durable your stand. By now what has not defeated is surely behind you and you will become the better for it.

Your bloom is where you can take pleasure in how you represent your blessings and how you can devise ways to bless others. At this point of your single season you are no longer fixated on you and your circumstances; you are more aware of how you can positively contribute to the lives you touch on a regular basis as well as those who pass your life as a test to your character and development.

I found a wonderful excerpt from a weekly E-devotional that I write. It goes out to over 14,000 people around the globe and it's called **Snack Food for the Soul**. You can subscribe to this e-mail by going to my website www.thepowerofperspective.net I will never share your email with anyone and I will never try to sell something. It's just a 90 second read to help put your mind in the right perspective for the week ahead. It will arrive at 12 midnight Monday morning every week until you unsubscribe. This topic is called:

SIMPLE MATH

One plus one equals two. One minus one equals zero. As children, these numerical facts served as the basis that helped us to calculate the simple things in life. As we grew older and more sophisticated we learned a different kind of math. We understood that people in our lives are like ocean waves on a beach; people are either adding to our lives or taking away. Most of us are too busy or not attentive enough to notice the significance of the people we have meals with, text, email or call on a regular basis.

Out of the ten people you encounter the most in a week, which are the ones that make a deposit and who are the ones who constantly withdraw? Certainly a healthy relationship will be a balance. This is a cooperative or mutually beneficial relationship. More than likely this relationship feels right for both parties. Then we have the type of relationship that causes stress to one or both parties. This is the kind of relationship where one benefits and the other suffers over a period of time. If you've ever been in one of these types of friendships, you have already begun to nod your head in agreement.

My life experiences have led me to understand that life will send you three types of people. The first type is the TAKER. They always want the spot light and the attention. Most importantly they want something from you and invariably bring a certain degree of drama along as garnish on their complicated platter. When they appear they want your undivided attention without reciprocating any prolonged interest in your life, unless it's in further exchange for even more of your attention.

If you begin to tell them you have a problem with a sharp pain in your side when you breathe deeply they immediately interrupt and begin their doctoral dissertation on the headache they get every afternoon at 2:30. God bless them, they are really harmless as long as you see them coming.

The second type of person is the one we all consider ourselves to be and that is the GIVER. The giver is the one who is always thinking of ways to be a blessing to the people they are about to encounter as well as the people they meet. Givers have a hard time receiving but will accept a blessing as long as it is not a hardship or inconvenience to the other person. Givers tend to be patient and listen carefully and try to find a means of assistance whenever possible. Givers seldom seek the spotlight

45

although a light always seems to follow them.

The third type is the easiest to describe. These individuals always seem to be on the fence. They neither take nor give. Their presence in your life is like the stranger that passes you by in the shopping mall and your eyes meet for a split second as you either nod in acknowledgement of each other or you ignore each other and keep going. These folks are still precious creations of God, but they just keep passing through our lives until their specific value to us materializes.

Jesus had givers and takers too. The givers had the least to say but the most to show. Take for instance the woman with the issue of blood. Her faith drove her on her belly to the hem of His garment and yet He was able to distinguish her touch from the throngs of people around Him.

The Centurion captured Jesus' heart by his belief in the Master's spoken word. The wisdom of Mary taking the time to sit at the master's feet pleased the Lord as Martha consumed herself with distraction. The next is the thief who hung on the cross next to Jesus simply said "Lord remember me when you come into your Kingdom."

The takers were just about everyone else who hung around Him including many of His disciples. Although they were in the very presence of the incarnation of God they still couldn't get it together. The interesting thing about this relationship is that they provided the Son of God with companionship.

He didn't need them for validation; His divinity did that for Him. He knew their strengths and weaknesses and assessed them daily. He knew the difference between tolerance and the need to care enough to confront. He knew there was a time to be in company and a time to be alone. He chose His friends, actions and journeys carefully because there was a purpose to each.

We too, should allow the divine assignment of balance and purpose to the relationships in our lives. As you contemplate the balance of GIVERS and TAKERS in your life; understand that as the righteousness of God we must have them both in order to be balanced ourselves.

Ecclesiastes 3:1-9 makes Simple Math even simpler: "A time to give birth, and a time to die; A time to plant, and a time to uproot what is planted. A time to kill, and a time to heal; A time to tear down, and a time to build up. A time to weep, and a time to laugh; A time to mourn, and a time to dance. A time to throw stones, and a time to gather stones; A time to embrace, and a time to shun embracing. A time to search, and a time to give up as lost; A time to keep, and a time to throw away. A time to tear apart, and a time to sew together; A time to be silent, and a time to speak. A time to love, and a time to hate; A time for war, and a time for peace."

This week, ask yourself; with all that's going on in this season of your life, are you GIVING, TAKING or just passing through?

CHAPTER THREE

LEARNING TO ACCEPT TRUTH

Once you embrace truth it will never sneak up on you, betray you or hide in the shadows of your mind. Jesus said I am the way, the truth and the life. Wherever you see the name Jesus in the word, change it to truth and the sentence will still have its meaning.

WHAT IS IT?

*H*ere's that quote again; you will find it in every book I write. *"Truth merits no reward, nor does it dignify a response. Truth is unimpeachable, therefore absolute.* Once you embrace truth at its very core, you will never be taken by surprise nor will you ever be betrayed. That is a strong statement for some to hear; even stronger for most to internalize. I'll begin by breaking it down this way. Anywhere you find the name Jesus or God in the bible you can substitute it with the words truth or love. There is truth in love and love in truth.

Most of us are programmed to believe that truth is a bad or a negative thing. Nothing could be further from the truth. The bible says the truth shall set you free. Truth is knowledge and knowledge is power. Those who fear truth are imprisoned by fear and ignorance. Fear and ignorance is the very reason that Christ's church has not progressed much beyond where He left it 2 millennia ago. ***Fear keeps us ignorant because we are comfortable knowing the little that keeps us safe and unchallenged.*** We know that the more we know the more accountable we shall have to become. After all, remaining the same is a lot easier than having to change or better yet, having to improve and grow.

So truth has gotten this bad reputation as something we should avoid at all costs. We see it in our western culture as brighter than the lights on Broadway. We call it polite conversation or being politically correct or (PC). We have actually become the hypocritical society that scorns people who actually speak what is on our minds.

 Its okay for us to think that masturbation is the acceptable if you are single and celibate for five years but we better not keep company with someone who is transparent enough to speak about it publically. If that's to forward or rude, how about the amount of times you have explored the fact that you are not sure how thin of a line there is between sanity and insanity?

How many times have you questioned your own sanity? Let's be real; we are all a little wacky in our own way. We just don't want anyone else to think of us that way. Because if they do, they will take it way to the other end of the pendulum and have us on the virtual brink of committal to the local psycho ward. So what do we do? We hide adjust and pretend the same way that we did in grade school, except now our methods are a bit more sophisticated because we picked up some great life skills from our hurts, our friends and too much TV.

THE CONSOLATION OF TRUTH

If you look at yourself as you stand there naked in the mirror and you come to the conclusion that you are overweight and you have stretch marks and puckered skin that looks like cottage cheese, then no one will ever be in the position to hurt your feelings again. Easier said than done you say? Well accept and hold closely. I'm not saying to identify yourself strictly by the way you look.

I'm saying that don't let the way you look drive you into a corner. Until the moment you decide that it is time to lose the weight, you should be able to see yourself as a spirit filled, positive and sexy woman. *Yes, you can be sexy and spirit filled at the same time.* You see, there is another word that we have become afraid of; especially in the church. That is part of the one-two punch of fear and ignorance. *Sexy doesn't only mean a vaginal length skirt, six inch stiletto heels, a blue wig and the nick name sunshine.*

The word sexy like the word beautiful is a perception by the beholder. For a man who is fairly psychologically balanced, there is nothing sexier than a woman who is certain of herself and free of hang-ups and insecurities. Some of the most stunning and sexy women I know are a little on the chunky side with the personality of an Ambassador. God and men want women who are comfortable in their skin and transparent.

If there is something that you are insecure about, come to terms with it. Just because it brings you displeasure doesn't mean that you should dis-credit it. There is a saying that you should keep your friends close and your enemies closer. If there is something about your life that you consider your enemy then you should deal with it in incremental portions as the reality it.

There is a woman that I will refer to as Sarah. She is a breath taking woman who I met while I was going through my first divorce. Our friendship consisted of several phone conversations and two dinner dates. I vividly recall taxi cabs and city buses slowing down as we would walk down the street.

The driver would slow down long enough to get a good look but not long enough to be disrespectful. She was used to it and knew how to not let it get to her. She was a dancer and actress who got a fair share of work on the New York "A" list.

As we got to know each other better she became more aloof and would seem to find reasons for us to not see each other. As an easy going type of guy, I politely gave her the opportunity to stop seeing each other entirely and that I would not take it personally. After all I was not looking for a serious relationship just someone to accompany me on job related social events. She quickly retorted that it was not me, but her past that keeps her from getting close to nice guys that remind her of her brothers.

You see Sarah was raped repeatedly by her brothers when she was sixteen. Although she knew I or any other man she met would mean her no harm, she couldn't get the fact out of her head that men are primarily sexual creatures. It didn't help that I vaguely resembled one of her brothers. I learned about resiliency from Sarah.

She ended up moving to Europe to pursue a lucrative modeling contract. Before she left she told me that the fact that she had been molested has nothing to do with me and unless she learns to get over this enemy within her past she will miss out on life. In her own words, I recall her saying that, *"I've got to get over myself and stop thinking that I am the only woman on earth this has happened to.*

This horrible act doesn't define me, but it is a part of my past. This past just happens to add more texture and dimension in my ability to reason and judge." That moment I saw a beautiful young lady become an incredible woman. Although she was beautiful on the outside she felt ugly and damaged. The mind is a powerful tool that can also become our most formidable obstacle.

Sarah knew that she had a valuable asset in her looks but she couldn't embrace it. Her looks were the catalyst for these heinous acts. We've spoken once since then and she was engaged to be married but felt the need to get in touch with me to let me know that she was healed and ready to move on. She said that I was the only man she had ever told about her past and so she felt accountable to me since I prayed with her and didn't judge her. Now that Sarah has embraced her truth it will never sneak up on her nor will it betray or deceive her.

So what is it about your life that has you running scared like Sarah? Perhaps there's nothing that has you gripped and manipulated as strongly as her past. Maybe it's a mole on your face, a tattoo or piercing that you had done on the whim of emotion. Maybe it is your weight or your unique body type.

Do you realize that we as the human species spend more time concerned about what others think about our situation than we ourselves? Here's an example. If I were to show you five full length pictures of five different women in bathing suits and asked you to guess what about their bodies made them insecure, how accurate do you think you would be?

We know one thing right away and that is you will impose your issues into your decision making. For instance if you hate your thighs, you will immediately look at hers. If you hate you're your hips you will immediately look at hers and so on. Here's the kicker.

Regardless what you feel are her insecurities, you will never know unless you meet that woman and she tells you for herself. The truth here is if you have an issue with hips, she may come from a culture where hips that are large and shapely are considered sexy and a part of a woman's crowning glory.

If this were the case then your guess would be completely wrong. Here's another example. Let's say another picture displayed a scar on the left cheek of one of the women. It would be a plain as the nose on your face that her scar should be the cause of her insecurity.

After talking with her she may reveal that she got that scar as she happened by her daughter's house whose date at the time was attempting to make a good night kiss more than the daughter wanted it to be. The mother got that scar while fighting off her daughter's attacker who may have easily raped her. To this day that mother considers her scar a badge of honor.

These scenarios are not made up by the way, they are true. But the purpose of using them is to illustrate that we project a lot of ourselves into the judgment calls we make on people. The other point is that most people tend to be more concerned about how others perceive them rather than how they perceive themselves. This is where a lot of confusion and anxiety is created. ***If we took a moment to consider that most people are not nearly as consumed with our imperfections as we are, we would all be happier people.***

Think about it. Most people are too consumed in themselves and their own lives to care about yours, so what makes you think that they care a single moment to try to figure out the intricate combination to the lock that gets you unraveled? When someone sees you they are seeing the total picture. They don't just see the mole on your face or your body type. They are seeing you from head to toe. Some people are so fixated on certain body parts they may never even see the whole you. I for one am so into teeth that as soon as someone starts to speak, that is the body part that I see the most of. Although as a public speaker, I know that I should look at your eyes, I will invariably end up staring in your mouth.

Remember the example of projection we just used. When they see you they may instantly notice your hair, your wonderfully flawless skin or your incredible smile. These may be the things that they feel they lack. *So now that they see you they are admiring or rejecting the things they have personal issues with.*

What's really funny is that the thing that you are most insecure about may not even come to their attention at all. They may be put off about the fact that you have natural finger nails and they can't grow theirs past nubs. Or better yet, the short and naturally curly hair that you have and adore may actually be a turn off to them because all their life they were told that short hair is ugly on women.

So the fact that you hate your skinny legs may be a positive thing to them simply for the fact that they think their legs are too fat. Do you see how pre-occupied with their own world people can be?

Unless you carry yourself in the manner that personifies your insecurity, no one will ever know. We all are like children who pretend. We don't want anyone to know the factors in our life that we have not gotten over. Guess what? You are not the only one. It's the same thing with the enemy. Satan can't read your mind. He really can't. He's not that powerful. He actually can't create anything. All he can do is mimic and pervert. What he can do successfully is surmise your thoughts according to your nature and track record. The bible says in (Psalms 51:5) *"Surely I was sinful at birth, sinful from the time my mother conceived me."* This means that the enemy knows our sinful nature because he created it. So he understands how we think as a result of hatred, anger, jealousy, fear and the multitude of carnal characteristics.

REHEARSE YOUR TRUTH

Regardless of what you dislike about yourself try to see this issue as something that isn't exactly the truth, but an example of perception. That physical characteristic may not be noticeable to someone else. If the physical issue is an obvious one then perhaps use your mirror as your personal Broadway stage. Am I advocating that you talk to yourself and rehearse various situations so that you'll know how to handle them when they arise?

The answer is absolutely. Why is it that the entertainment world rehearses to entertain flawlessly for that which isn't real but we leave our lives and real life situations to chance?

It is perfectly normal to think situations through so that we can make sound decisions about our value system and our reasoning. *We should be able to take time to fully understand what makes us tick with the precision of a Swiss watch and what makes us implode like a house of cards.* Running from your fears and insecurities is like spending money and not knowing what's in your bank account because you are scared of running out of money. If God forbid you fell down and hit your head and lost your long term memory, chances are you would also forget that thing about you that haunts you so frequently.

Do you see how your issue is something you have to remember for it to haunt you? In my book, *Bruised Yet Priceless* I explain how holding onto resentment and anger is like clutching onto three pennies in your dominant hand. You cannot ever let go of these pennies. You just go through life shaking hands, washing yourself, feeding and caring for yourself as you hold onto these pennies.

Even when you sleep you must manage to hold onto those pennies. If they fall out of your hand, you must wake yourself and find them so that you won't lose them. They must be there when you wake up. So these pennies can even cost you a good night's sleep, which interferes with your rest in your season of singleness.

Everyone can see your handicap as you compensate and over compensate for this condition. It becomes un-natural in ways, but because you give yourself no other choice, this must now remain your reality.

A penny is the least of denominational values. It makes up 1/100th of the U.S. dollar and is comprised of zinc and copper, which has little intrinsic value. *But after your self-inflicted need to hold onto this issue of pennies your hand which is symbolic of your life, your character and your faith will become deformed. This almost worthless penny can now almost cost you all that you own, including your peace of mind and personal freedom.*

So let's say that your fear or your insecurity is that thing that you are holding onto. Although what you are dealing with cannot be trivialized down to a penny, you still must face the fact that God invested the life of His Son into your life because of the high value of your destiny.

So getting back to that bump on your head that you got from the fall that caused you long term memory loss; do you realize that simply forgetting about it can make the pain go away? How much longer do you want to hold onto that pain, resentment, insecurity or that memory?

It doesn't define you and no one but you is making you a slave to it. Why not simply decide today to let that go. You're not alone. The Lord is the inspiration for this book, not me. I have no judgment or indictment for you and you know He certainly doesn't either. I don't know you and wish nothing but God's ultimate power and peace over every area of your life.

In a moment we will pray together and believe that the Spirit of the Lord will place His hand over yours as your teacher or parent once did when teaching you to write and comfort you with the courage and faith to loosen the grip of worthless burdens.

Here is where your rehearsal begins. At this point I suppose you thought that being single was simply that; a state of being. Not at all my friend. *Being single is an opportunity and a planned respite from having to be something to somebody other than yourself and perhaps your children if you are also a single parent.* There are things in your life like your weight, body type and socio-economic status that form your lifestyle that you may not be able to change right away. But you can certainly change your state of mind or mind style immediately.

There is a notion that I share in every one of my books that speaks to your thought life. Your thoughts are the most personal thing you own. Everything you think is completely between you and God. If God forbid you were to get your pocketbook and I.D. stolen then the perpetrator can use your credit cards and checkbook to assume your identity.

The wonderful thing is they cannot ever assume your thoughts. Even if you are still trying to recover from that head injury we spoke of earlier where you lost your long-term memory and you couldn't remember your mom and dad's name. You would still have your thoughts. So you see that thoughts are a powerful thing. If you work hard to change the way you think and respond then you will change.

Here are some rehearsal tips that may be helpful in you changing the way you think about the issues that haunt you:

1. Look yourself in the mirror and practice smiling when you say hello. Practice saying "hello and how are you doing today?" Say it with certainty and sincerity. If you have always been shy and lacked confidence in your greeting of someone, this is where you would have already lost the battle of making a good first impression. If you accomplish your greeting with certainty and sincerity no one will ever know what you has hung up.

2. Get on the internet and look up the top 10 fears and insecurities that people have. Get to know what they are and the causes for them. This will help your understanding of the fact that we as people all have some something that makes a rattling sound when we get shaken. That rattling sound shows that there is something that either needs tightening or it fell out of place. It doesn't mean that the device doesn't work, it just means that it has something peculiar going on. *You are not alone we all have something peculiar in the way we rattle. We just don't want anyone to know about it.*

3. Anonymity is how the enemy of man operates. He has a way of isolating us in a corner just like that grade school bully that pushed around the boys you knew. If the enemy can isolate your thoughts to where you think that it's just you, then he can isolate the way you speak and behave. The enemy likes to keep us ignorant. So by empowering your mind you will see that you are not alone, nor are you deficient. At least once a day while

you are at work and at home; in fact every mirrored rest room you enter, tell yourself in the mirror that "there is nothing wrong with me. In fact I'm normal and that makes me unique." *Hearing your voice speak to your soul in the places that you are not free to be totally transparent will encourage you.*

4. Truth is a two way street. Don't just embrace the bad, learn to celebrate the good. Even if the only things you absolutely love about yourself are your ear lobes and your high arches. Wear some great high heels and fabulous ear rings that grab every pair of eyes that come your way. *Practice that walk that exudes confidence and that tilt of your head that says "I know". Remember that you are a woman. God made you to show mankind His artistic flair. You are a piece of art.*

5. If the thing you love most about yourself is not tangible at all but emanates from your eternal soul such as your ability make people laugh or your skill with words that bring life to any solemn situation; then you need to let her free so you along with everyone else in the room can kick off your heels and sit back and enjoy the show.

    You know what I mean. If you have one of those electrifying personalities that enters the room like a cool fragrant filled summer breeze, then baby let that wind blow and show the world that you are a creature of God who is well familiar with the wit, the humor and the presence of God.

6. Be honest about how you could be perceived. Nothing should surprise you. If you are insecure about the fact that you are always late then don't get offended when people tease or comment about your bad habit. If you are

known for something about yourself that isn't positive but you are responsible for creating that label, then you should either change it immediately or accept it and give up the sensitivity about it. You're a woman now and part of being such is accepting the negatives in life with strength and humility until you either change direction in your storm or until the storm passes. No one wants to hear your complaints.

7. *Jesus said "In everything give thanks" (1 Thessalonians 5:18) KJV. He didn't say FOR everything give thanks, but IN everything give thanks.* The secret to feeling God's pleasure over you is by unconditionally loving and thanking Him for all areas of your life. Have you ever felt like you were taken for granted? How do you think the Lord feels when we only give Him glory and thanksgiving in the good times, but we ignore Him and question Him in the bad times?

None of these are earth-shattering facts, but if you pattern them together you have the making of a change in mind style which will invariably change your life style. Many of us spend enough time rehearsing arguments and going over comments that we made as a result of comments that were made to us. *Now here we are reliving and acting out an argument that took place days and weeks ago.* To add insult to injury we get upset and worked up all over again. Isn't it time we stop rehearsing the negative and start rehearsing the positive. Bad news comes whether we want it or not. Bad news doesn't care if you are eating, sleeping, taking a shower or in a good mood or not. Like the rain, bad news comes when it's good and ready.

Why are we rehearsing bad news and asking God to finally send us some good news. From the outside looking in, one could easily surmise that we are truly crazy. The fact is, as long as we allow the enemy and his mindset to take up residence in our spirit and steal our joy then we really are crazy. We are actually losing our mind to the enemy.

Just like bad news, he doesn't care where you are. When police officers come looking to serve an arrest warrant, they don't care if you're doing your nails, taking a shower or just about to put your kids to bed. They will come busting through your door to take care of business. The enemy seeks to do the same.

He knows his time is running out and he just wants to take as many of us with him as possible. So let's not mimic his hatred for us by self-destructing and talking condemnation to our lives and the people we love. Let's rehearse life and life more abundantly. Change your mind style; change your words by changing the intent of your heart.

The best way of showing God how you hate the enemy is by resisting him. Don't give in so easily to the predictable ways of the enemy. He knows you're mad. He knows you're offended. So does the Lord and all the angelic hosts. They're all waiting to see what you are going to do. The bible says in (James 4:7), *Submit yourselves therefore to God. Resist the devil, and he will flee from you."*

The scripture didn't say, curse out the one who behaves like the devil. The scripture didn't say, get on the phone and murmur to your entire contacts list stored in your phone. *The word said resist as in restrain yourself from what comes naturally and the devil will see that restraint as the power of God and he will be forced to flee from the authority of God.*

Here is where we pray. The prayers in this book and all the Power of Perspective series are prayers that you can personalize and internalize into your life. Say them regularly if prayer is not a part of your daily routine until you have the confidence to say them with authority and consistency.

"Father, you know that I've been broken for some time and that I've noticed it too. I thought that by not coming clean with you and deciding to change would make it less painful. Lord, the fact is that I am tired of being broken down without being broken for you. Lord, I need to be fixed and I'm tired of the burden of pride, hurt, resentment, shame and fear.

Sometimes I don't even know which one I'm feeling on a given day. Father, please take this rattle out of my spirit, please remove the obstacles in my life that keep me from serving you. Remove my taste for the sinful nature and the sinful acts that torment me before and even after I commit them. Let me have the obedience and courage to conform to your will for my life. I'm tired of making mistakes and wasting time that I could be happy and fulfilled in your will.

I know that this is your desire for me and I know that I have been disobedient. Lord, please forgive me for not wanting to listen to you and please forgive me for my pride and the falsehood in my character. Lord, please wash me in your blood and make me whole and ready for your service.

Lord, I know that you are my Savior and I know that your son, Jesus died for me and I know that your precious Holy Spirit desires to live in me and guide me. Lord, I know that eternity with you is my destiny. Father, please stand up within me so I can forgive myself and my posture for you will be upright and respectable in your eyes and mine, in Jesus name. Amen."

CHAPTER FOUR
CHANGE YOUR MIND

Changing your mind and deciding to look at something differently should be as easy as saying, "I want to feel better about something in my life that I cannot change. I deserve to feel better because Christ has invested His life in my joy."

THE HIDDEN COSTS

$\mathcal{I}$n chapter three we briefly discussed the intrinsic value of your thoughts and how what you think of yourself can undermine your destiny. Here is where we find the shoe that fits. One of the first things that will bring you a sense of completeness and personal freedom is your willingness to also let go of your sensitivities.

I'm not saying that you need to let go of your sensitivities that are relative in showing compassion or tenderness to others, I'm saying that sometimes we as people embrace sensitivities that are not part of the purchase price for the ticket to our destiny. Unnecessary sensitivities become those annoying additional fees we see on our utility and cell phone bills.

Those annoying additional costs add up. When you look at the initial phone bill that is $92.35 it's not that bad. But when you follow the numbers down the column through the additional surcharges, taxes and so on, your bill is now $132.45. What happened to the $92.35 worth of services that you actually used? The company and the government exercise their right to bill you for infrastructure usage, administrative costs and simply for the fact that you are breathing air. I say that to be funny of course, but from our point of view that seems to be the rationale behind the fees.

Many of us are guilty of charging ourselves unnecessary fees as well. Think about it; when you allow yourself to get offended simply the way someone looks at you, speaks to you, or by the way they carry themselves. Then like the issue of the lack of forgiveness, you are causing yourself unnecessary hardship and burden.

Just like those fees, they don't make it impossible to afford a phone but it would make life easier if they weren't there. By going through life as a sensitive or easily offended person doesn't make your life an impossible one to live but it makes it just that much more difficult to fulfill.

We all have issues in life that set us off in a completely different emotional direction than planned. There you are walking down life's path minding your own business and all of a sudden there it is, that object in your path that you cannot pass by. Many on the path with you will simply step over, around or even step through is despite the consequences. In either case these individuals are not bothered or distracted by the object. Then here comes beautiful, unique and irresistible you. As soon as you see the object you stop, stare and completely allow your mental and emotional bias toward this object to envelop you.

You become so taken by this object that the entire world comes to a complete stand still. Now let's give this scenario some dimension and texture so it's more for you. Here's a scenario: a girlfriend of your invites you to an event. Since you like more specifics, let's say it's a wedding.

You arrive a little late and everyone is already seated so you are on a slight edge since you now have to climb over people to get to the only available seats in the middle of the church. You consider just standing in the back in a corner but you realize that would be disrespectful to the bride since you don't even know her.

The wedding begins and you and your girlfriend settle in and do your final primping so that you look good if you happen to show up in the wedding video. You feel a bit uneasy as you admire the ornate church fixtures and beautiful colors.

You casually and instinctively glance over your left shoulder and there is a pair of ominous eyes staring at you menacingly. It's as if she knows you well enough to give you this stare. You realize that you have never seen her before and quickly take offense to her gaze. The wedding begins and every now and then you look toward your new nemesis and she continues to give you the evil eye. You have become so irritated that you can almost feel your body temperature begin to rise.

You can't even hear the beautiful vows that the new couple to be is sharing with the on lookers. Then you hear a collective awe and your girlfriend and every woman around you begins to cry. You become so consumed by the evil gaze you are getting that you completely miss the beautifully romantic gesture the groom just made. Now you're even more upset.

Later at the reception you and your girlfriend are standing and talking and all of a sudden an unfamiliar voice calls out your girlfriend's name and she quickly turns around. As if fate and humor connect at your feet, you encounter face to face the person you would like to have some choice words with for making you miserable throughout the entire wedding ceremony.

She and your girlfriend share a quick embrace and casual brush of the cheek and then she introduces you. She already has a smug look on her face because she knows that she has gotten to you. She conveniently miss-pronounces your name as she hears your girlfriend clearly say your name. She barely shakes your hand and rolls her eyes at you. Your girlfriend and everyone else in the room are oblivious to the private war being waged between your ears. You excuse yourself and go to the ladies room to cool off.

So, what just happened can either be typical or extremely rare in your life. The answer totally depends on you. Although very specific, the premise of the story is that if you are the woman being stared at then you easily allow people to get into your head and take up residence there. It can be as specific as these circumstances or as random as a lightning strike. Some women are put off by someone bumping into them accidentally and not saying "I'm sorry" at all or maybe the apology was not sincere enough. Maybe you easily get caught up in the fact that no one pays you any attention when you walk into the room. Better yet let's make a list. Let's call this list, "you know you're too sensitive when"

1. You get upset when you see another woman wearing the same outfit as you.
2. Someone is dressed inappropriately for an event and it bothers you the whole evening
3. You are used to being the focus of all attention but tonight there is even one more fair than you in the kingdom and she is getting all the attention
4. You over hear someone saying something to someone else and by the way they look at you, you feel that they are talking about you.
5. The usual stare from a stranger puts you in a bad mood

If any one of these situations has occurred to you and caused you some stress then you are too sensitive. *Sensitivity is a good thing when it comes to expressing compassion to others, but it's a bad thing when it causes you anxiety and mood swings. By seeing and holding onto things that are simply a matter of perspective can cost you friendships, relationships and peace of mind.* No one likes to be around someone with a whole bunch issues that easily get blown out of proportion. Do you remember the nursery rhyme "Sticks and Stones may break my bones but names will never hurt me?" Now that you are an adult who is single, this is where you should have the time to change your mind about the things that get to you.

Just like choosing to forgive someone, you can also choose to not allow petty items like the aforementioned list to pollute your mind with negativity and destructive thinking. Half the people on this planet are trying to get to the same destination... fulfillment. The distinguishing factor between them is only half in search of self-fulfillment will actually find it.

Most want the destination but have no clue as to how to get there. There is a road map to self-fulfillment but most don't have the proper directions. Do you? The purpose of this book once again is to help you to become complete while you are by yourself instead of looking for a man to complete you.

If you have personal joy then you are guaranteed to have self-fulfillment. Notice, I didn't say if you have happiness you have self-fulfillment. Happiness is based on circumstances, but joy is your nature. Here is an excerpt from my weekly devotional called *Snack Food for the Soul*. The topic for this particular thought is:

HAPPINESS IS YOUR MOOD; JOY IS YOUR NATURE

Have you ever encountered someone who was in worse shape than you but somehow they managed to cheer you up? Imagine visiting someone in the hospital or in hospice care who should be so down and out but there is a spark that comes from within them that seems to catch on and warms you all over. On the flip side our world is filled with folks who have millions of dollars in the bank yet their lives appear as big and empty mansions that are emotionally and spiritually bankrupt.

It seems like every few weeks we hear about our Western culture's version of royalty; our Hollywood "A list", our mega million price tagged athletes and our iconic singers. One from each category has slipped up again and done one of the very things that our parents warned us not to do when we were children.

We utter to ourselves that "if we had their money, we would never cause so much problems. We would pay off our bills and live quietly under the radar. Imagine how much joy we could bring our loved ones with ten million dollars in the bank."

Ah, there's a funny thing about the words happiness and joy. They are so similar but their difference can literally mean life and death. Happiness is often tied to someone's state of mind characterized conditionally by love, work, family, social status and proximity to other happy people. Joy on the other hand is one's ability to be content and at peace despite the external conditions mentioned.

In my 20 plus years in media and ministry I have encountered some of the wealthiest celebrities, politicians, surgeons and even ambassadors who never cracked a smile or had a kind word to say about anyone or anything. Yet I have sat in the company of the impoverished and homeless who were so hospitable you would think they were real estate developers.

I sat by the bedside of the terminally ill who smiled and looked back at their brief life like it were a wonderful nursery rhyme filled with smiles and familiar melodies. I've encountered victims of horrible crimes who were as quick to embrace and forgive their perpetrators as they would forgive their own child for breaking a toy.

What is this wonderful resource that these remarkable people share? It's a comforting old friend called joy, joy, joy. What is the source of this joy? Jesus. There is now research called the Psychology of Happiness, and at the core of these studies is one's spirituality. Joy is the assurance and richness you feel deep within despite the deficit in your bank account.

Joy is that invisible umbrella that seems to shield you through the most difficult storms in your life. Joy is the warm smile you greet everyone with that enters your hospital room despite the doctor's report. Joy is the identity you still have and the purpose you still feel the need to pursue despite the fact you are suddenly unemployed.

Joy is the embrace and forgiveness you extend when your pride and your emotions tell you to react otherwise. Joy tells you to pick up the phone and cheer someone up even though you just received some bad news.

Joy tells you to say good morning to the valley of dead bones who may be your co-workers or family members even though they won't say it in return. Happiness is a shy individual who only comes out on her own conditions. She will be the smiling patient but the prognosis needs to be a good one. She may show on the face of the celebrity, the homeless and the ones we love, but their needs to be some conditions attached.

These conditions need to be fulfillment in love, work, family, good health, status and the proximity to other happy people. The need for these criteria doesn't make her a bad person at all, they simply need to be around so that she is at her best and others may get the benefit of her company.

Joy and happiness are great together but you can certainly have joy when the happenstance that supports happiness is taken away. Joy will make you want to stick around to see what's around the corner even though you've been through a tough season.

Joy will encourage you to not let a rough season become your climate. When you feel beat down and discouraged, joy will remind you of something miraculous in your past that will connect you to something amazing about your present. The smile that comes to your face will appear like the sunset that amazes all who surround you.

Joy is a chain reaction that is truly contagious because of the healing virtue of its transparency. Happiness may change your mood but joy can change your nature.

Perspective is a powerful concept. Once you learn that everything you encounter can be viewed from different vantage points, you begin to see things other than just the way you've chosen to see them in the past. You can choose to be joy filled and you can choose to not let petty things and petty people get to you.

If you come across a man who has his act together and you don't, then he will see you as a project that needs undertaking and you will be labeled as needy. *Men do not want needy women. They want women who are happy, secure, intelligent and baggage free.* Sometimes we take ourselves and the lives we think we lead a little too seriously. We should all from time to time break free from all the masks that we wear in order to get through the day and just look at ourselves and either have a good laugh or a good cry about how the roles we play rule our lives.

At the end of the day, the Lord does not care nor is He impressed about the way you look, the tax bracket you are represented by or how good you look. All of these factors are opportunities that His grace and mercy has afforded you. Jesus is not moved by status, He is moved by how we handle ourselves in the most inopportune circumstances with the most difficult people who need Him just as much as we do.

THE HEALTHY CHOICE

Choosing to not allow things and people to bother you can also lead to a longer and more fulfilling life. Medical science proves that a positive and healthy state of mind can quite literally make or break your life. This is how it works. First of all I strongly suggest you also purchase the book, *The Biology of Belief by Bruce H. Lipton, Ph.D.* Dr. Lipton is a cell biologist and medical school professor. His groundbreaking studies have revolutionized the way that the medical industry and the scientific community look at the way we think and the way we conceptualize spirituality.

At our most basic level of existence which is our blood cells, we can begin changing. Modern science has told mankind that our DNA make up determines our fate and our functional levels. New research has proven that this is no longer true. Our cells are created with a degree of instinct and intelligence despite the fact that they have no brains they can decide good from bad. Studies have concluded that if you take a single cell and place it in a petri dish and place a protein on the right side of the petri dish and a toxin on the other side; the single cell will begin to move toward the protein to feed itself.

When you place another cell in the same petri dish, they instinctively move toward each other and then move toward the protein. On our most basic level of existence our cells are motivated to join together and pool their resources in order to survive. In spite of what our birth circumstances may say, we are not pre-disposed to fail.

73

The human genome which is the architectural drawings or the DNA make-up of humans actually changes. Despite what your genetic pre-disposition dictates at birth, 20 years later they can completely change. An infant at 3 months of age will have a completely different genome when he is 20 years of age.

This answers the question that many of us ask. Can I really change if my mother has always been this way and her mother's mother and so on? The answer is an absolute yes according to this new research. As spirit filled believers of Christ we already know that when the Holy Spirit has come upon you that you will receive power according to (Act 1:8). What this new research is showing proves that *"Therefore, there is now no condemnation for those who are in Christ Jesus."* (Romans 8:1). Even the body has no condemnation to offer you once you make up your mind to be the very best available vessel for Christ that you can be. Now say this, "I can Change." Say it again, "I can change."

Now say, *"I am capable in deciding to change by no longer allowing myself to be distracted and agitated by circumstances and people who have nothing to do with my destiny in the Lord."* Now think back in your life and consider the amount of times that you have actually said words to yourself that can actually bring peace and restoration instead of anxiety and frustration.

How many times have you actually rehearsed an argument that you just knew that you were going to have with someone. As mentioned before, it's time to rehearse for where you are going not where you are trying to depart. Don't look back to Sodom and Gomorrah.

Be like Lot and not his wife (Gen 19:26), *But Lot's wife looked back, and she became a pillar of salt*. God sent Angels to rescue them from a city that was destined for destruction due to its evil ways and perversions. Lot and his wife were warned by the angels to purify their minds and hearts and to not look back or they would turn to a pillar of salt. Lot's wife could not let go of her comfort zone and was stuck in her belief system and as a result was literally frozen in her beliefs as she turned to stone and perished. You can't change how people behave and treat you, but you can certainly control how they affect you. You have the power to control your reactions not them. There is a saying that you cannot stop the birds from flying over your head, but you can keep them from setting up a nest in your hair.

Fear is another aspect of life that we can choose to conquer or allow it to overtake our lives. The following fear section is taken from the book that inspired the entire Power of Perspective brand and book series, The Power of Perspective book one.

Don't be afraid of truth

"You're fat and your mother dresses you funny", everybody bursts into laughter and the fat, strangely attired child goes running home to mommy. Ever heard this before? How about, "Yo momma is so fat, when she goes to the beach the Coast Guard goes on alert to rescue beached whales". Here's a cute one, "Yo momma is so short, she can sit on a dime and dangle her legs".

 In African-American culture it is referred to as the "Dozens", "Dirty Dozens" or "Ranking". This is a competition generally among males where they would quickly recite these witty, untrue insults against each other's family members until the other has run out of responses. The "Yo momma" jokes are usually the crowd favorite.

This later evolved into the hip hop culture where rappers would battle each other using the same witty recitations but applying the digging insults to the opposition's rapping style. By the end of each competition, there is generally a winner and a loser. In most cases, all parties walk away with some laughs and new responses for the next challenge.

Rarely are there any real words exchanged to genuinely harm the other's pride or family. However, in life, there is always someone who searches out our weaknesses to use against us in a public display of infantile behavior. For some of us, these efforts are futile, while with others, these words can prove to be very hurtful.

The bible says, *"You will know the truth and the truth will make you free"* (John 8:32). Although Jesus was referring to the fact that knowing the truth about Him will make us free from the bondage of sin, one can easily make the correlation that knowing the truth about your life and your circumstances will make you free from fearing them.

Those of us who are sensitive about our appearance find great pain when the subject comes up for criticism or when we are the brunt of careless jokes. But understanding that being overweight is seen by everyone as an issue one should embrace until it is able to be remedied by diet and exercise or medical intervention, can make all the difference.

The same goes for those of us who have features that are not looked upon as aesthetically pleasing to those around us. We should simply embrace that as a reality that we must bear. You see, when you take an inward journey into yourself, you will not only find the wreckage, but you will also find the buried treasure. If you are overweight, you should also discover that you are more wonderful to be around than a skinny and moody individual who is so starch and protein deprived that their brain can't sort their emotions. Although that is said in jest, you should embrace your strengths and weaknesses equally so neither takes complete control of your existence.

This is called balance. *You should glean energy from your strengths and allow your weaknesses to keep you grounded; otherwise, you will be unstable and irrelevant.* No one should ever be able to knock you off balance by throwing a negative fact about you in your face. I can be brutally honest at times when necessary and as gentle as a lamb as well. I can also take brutal honesty about my ways. Always be able to handle what you dish out and always be prepared to hold yourself accountable to what you expect from others.

Growing up, I never felt that I was as cool or good looking as the friends that I hung out with and they used to remind me of that every now and then when we played the Dozens. I quickly developed a quick wit and sharp tongue, and eventually won most ranking sessions. I had great confidence because the girlfriends of most of my friends trusted me as their best friend and I always had the upper hand because I had the personality everyone wanted to be around.

I always knew that my people skills were my gift even though I had low self-esteem overall. Whatever is a sensitive area in your life, embrace it like your name and become well acquainted with it so that it no longer causes you anxiety. Some people grew up very poor and are ashamed of it and when any issue concerning economics comes up, they become sensitive and defensive. This is nothing to be ashamed of. You should see this as another factor that completes the dimensions of your character, not a thorn in your side.

The fact that my mother and father were never married used to bother me tremendously, so   I used to tell my friends that my mom and dad were divorced when I was very young. One day, one of my friends jokingly called me a bastard and I quickly retorted by saying, "How did you know that my dad and mom were never married"? That stole her thunder, but cured me of that sensitivity.

Comedians learn to laugh at their own pain and find healing through making others laugh in the process. Try to look at your malady, upbringing, appearance or whatever it is that you are sensitive about in a holistic manner. Don't see it as what you are summed up as, look at it as one of the things you are known for.

If you are comfortable about it, then the world around you will too. I had an English teacher in grade school that had a deformed hand and students who were not in his class would see him and look away in embarrassment and ask students in his class if he was strange or mean. I happened to be one of his students and would say that he is one of the coolest teachers I've ever had.

You see this teacher we'll call Mr. Martin, came in on the first day of class and introduced himself and told us all about his background. Then he said, "Oh, by the way, you will notice that my hand only has four fingers and although it is deformed, you will see that I can write with it as well as shake your hand. Don't be afraid of it or me, we don't bite. However, be nice to this hand because it is the hand I write with when I grade test results and report cards". We all laughed and that was the end of the stares and prejudice.

At times I tend to be a bit particular about the fact that I tend to be germaphobic. But if someone takes a jab at me about it, I simply laugh it off because I know it is true. I also tend to be very verbal and obsessive about good communication and in fact I even poke fun at myself so others know not to take me too seriously when I banter on.

If you embrace the truth about yourself, it will never take you unaware or lead you astray. My mantra is that truth will never lie to you and will always be consistent with you. He will never be late; he will always clean up after himself and will never talk behind my back.

Truth is my best friend because he is always there to remind me of who I am despite what others say about me. Ladies, feel free to reverse truth's gender. The better you embrace truth, the more you will appear to be authentic in your presentation. If you appear transparent, then it is easier for someone to see the Jesus within. Proverbs 3:3 says, "Let not mercy and truth forsake you; Bind them around your neck, Write them on the tablet of your heart, And so find favor and high esteem, In the sight of God and man.

Don't be afraid of silence

We've all gotten used to an instantaneous society where we get what we want quicker and more conveniently. We can order online or by automated phone services. Most automated services get the job done without us having ever to speak to a live person. It's all about getting the job done faster. Many times when I get to a cashier, there isn't even a hello and eye contact, unless I initiate it.

I muse at the shock I give some cashiers when I say hello and refer to them by the name on their name tag. Remember what life was like before microwaves? We actually had to wait for something to warm for 20 or 30 minutes in a toaster oven or a conventional oven. I don't even remember what we did with the time while we were waiting. Nowadays, if my dual core high powered laptop takes longer than 10 seconds to open a program or application I'm ready to lose it.

We have rapidly become a society of immediate gratification and impatience. It's the old adage our parents used to tell us about society being bent on quantity over quality. Our churches are even marketing shorter sermons and church services so we can get in and out and get on with our day.

I am amazed to see churches that have early Sunday morning services so we can "get it out of the way". So how do we get God to maneuver His schedule and synchronize His eternal clock to our wrist watch or PDA? The fact is that we can't and He won't. God is not the least bit moved or impressed with what we do for a living, how much money and real estate we own, what we drive or even how many letters we've accumulated behind our last name.

God is more moved by the hungry homeless man who sacrifices a hand out to another homeless man who has less than he. God is moved by worship, faith, the selfless expression of love and forgiveness. All of these take time to cultivate. God does not move or reveal Himself in confusion. The primary reason law enforcement issues speeding tickets is to get our attention to a problem that we have with speeding and our potential to wreck our lives and the lives of others. God has a way of getting our attention to slow down as well. We call these tickets trials and storms. They also tend to give us patience.

The silence in our lives is the spaces between the noises that allow us to hear from God without interruption. These are the times that you really get the opportunity to flex your intimacy with God. Quietness with God is when you receive your instructions for battle. Being alone with God illuminates your path. *Have you ever been in a room full of people and felt as though if you instantly disappeared no one would even notice?*

Are there times that you feel this while with your loved ones or co-workers? Well this is why prayer and silence with God is critical. During this silent time with God, you are authorizing the creator of the universe to empower your spirit with His power to discern the heart of those around you so you would not be easily misled.

 Silence with God empowers you with the ability to overcome sickness and depression. Silence with God empowers you to have faith through financial hardship. *Here's the best part, silence with God completes you, and so you are no longer in need of anyone to fill your emptiness with hours of empty and meaningless conversations with people who really don't care about you or your purpose.*

 Some of us fear silence more than ridicule, because during silence there are no stimulior distraction from the outside, just the true honest image of ourselves and the world we have created. In many cases, this form of judgment is either uncomfortably unfamiliar or too harsh and cold. This is because in most cases, we have never been taught to take the time to honestly get to know ourselves as we are and as other people see us. We only want to know ourselves as how we think we portray our role in life. Here is a pivotal moment in our quest of not only intimacy within ourselves, but intimacy with God. This is where the building despite its beautiful façade says to the architect that I may need to be gutted and remade according to the original blueprints because I have more form than function.

When you want to hear from God on a certain issue, you must be silent without a time frame or agenda. You cannot determine on Wednesday morning at 10:30 a.m. that you will be silent and expect God to fully disclose all His wisdom to you on this topic by the end of your lunch hour. We can't have a deadline because that deadline might be intertwined with an agenda on what answer we are expecting from Him. God may require a few things from us first.

We need to be prepared with the fact that God wants our spirit clear of the anxiety at hand and wants to see us fully submitted to him. God knows why we are coming to Him. If He jumped as quickly as we asked, then He would be diminished to the father who is used by his spoiled little child who comes to Him with affection only when they want something.

During this broken time, we need to be cognizant of God's omniscience. God is all powerful and answers to no one but Himself. Our circumstances and the bad choices we made to get into these circumstances are of no significance to Him. He is the God who heals the sick and raises the dead. He is the God who can stop time. He is the God who also did not deliver the children of Israel to the Promised Land until an entire generation of those who disobeyed him, died. God knows the day we will see Him face to face.

His thoughts and ways are above our ways. With that said and understood, God will move when our spirit is settled and in full agreement with His power. When we are complete in this conflict within ourselves, not only will the circumstances seem smaller, He will also speak to our heart concerning matters.

Much like the homeless man, this is when you've got God's attention. As I've looked back over my life and assessed the damages I've created, I realize I could have avoided most, if not all of the chaos if I only took the time to be silent before making a harsh decision.

During my 20's I was married, had a demanding ministry as a broadcaster, had a career as a talk show producer, all while I completed my undergrad and graduate degrees full time. I certainly didn't take nearly the amount of time needed to be silent. *This lack of silence fueled the fleshly influences in my life causing me to make bad decisions. I can probably fill volumes of books with what those mistakes were.* One of those mistakes was divorcing my first wife and giving up my broadcast ministry to hundreds of thousands of people every week, the two most important things to me.

Upon the opening of my eyes every day, I do not allow myself to make one move out of bed without giving the Lord at least 15 minutes of total silence just to hear His heart. My times for worship are during my morning and evening shower. I also make it a habit to fall on my face at least once a day in worship and again after our daily family devotion and bedtime prayers.

Prayer, praise and worship are also woven into every activity I do during the day. For instance, as I sit and write at my computer, while I'm driving, working out at the gym or even playing ball with my kids, I am constantly saying, "Thank you Jesus or I bless your name Lord". For some, this ritual may be considered to be a luxury or a bit excessive, but my goal is greatness in God by any means necessary.

I did not have a lot of the nurturing mommy and daddy time as a child, so I made a lot of decisions without wise and sage parental counsel as a foundation. My contention is not to repeat the same mistakes over and over again. Success in silence is accomplished this way.

ASSIGNMENT

1. Clear your spirit of all malice, agendas and selfish desires by repenting.

2. Go to God in prayer and have the patience to be silent until He speaks purpose to your circumstance. Waiting for God to speak is a must.

3. Understand that sometimes the answer is so obvious that we cause our own delays by compounding our mental issues into God's clear and decisive plan. At other times, He may take longer because He wants us to just slow down. Our God has numbered the hairs on our head, so it stands to reason that He cares about us and our well-being.

4. When you receive confirmation in your spirit that your answer is from God, ask Him for the spirit of obedience that it will take to do that He says. A good clue that your answer is from God is that Satan will never ask you to do the Godly thing or something that denies your flesh of its gratification.

5. You will need the courage to execute God's plan for your circumstance simply because His answer may not be what you expected or what you truly want to do.

6. Ask God to give you the faith that says you know that His answer for your circumstance is going to work out for your good and that it will ultimately prove to be the best answer for your purpose.

7. Make sure to give God His due thanksgiving and praise for what He has done faithfully in your life.

Don't be afraid of change or struggle

For nine months or 40 weeks, a fetus floats innocently and safely in the amniotic fluid of its mother's womb. After nature evolves her body into a viable baby with functioning lungs, she must now begin to transition to her next level of development.

The ultimate success of this next shift in her development can only occur in most cases when there is great stress and trauma to her life. In fact, every aspect of her existence will be challenged as she enters the birth canal. Her skull, shoulders, rib cage and lungs are squeezed to half their size to accommodate this small entry way to her new universe. At this point, she must succumb to even more trauma of being cold, touched by hands for the very first time, filling her lungs with air and then having to scream in a room filled with bright lights. If that is not the text book definition of change and struggle, then we all need to start all over again.

The interesting thing about this necessary change is that if the baby does not make this transition into the outside world through the birth canal or cesarean section, she will go into distress and cause great risk or even death to her and her mother. Once a baby reaches full-term, the mother's body or its present surroundings begin to reject the baby.

It simply has outgrown its surrounding and it is time to leave. Much like a vine-ripened fruit or vegetable, once its time of development has been reached, it is either picked or drops to the ground. All truths are parallel, meaning that what happens in the spiritual realm also happens in the natural realm.

When you reach a place spiritually and God has decided that it is time for you to move on, you will start to feel uncomfortable with where you are. You will start to see signs in your everyday interactions; things that seemed to flow just won't seem the same anymore. In the case of the newborn, all hell starts to break loose. Unless you have graduated from the class of not fearing silence, you won't see it coming. God will make you uncomfortable with where you are (complacency) to get you to where you need to be (destiny).

A dear friend of mine by the name of Bishop Noel Jones once taught me that you must be willing to let go of the past in order to firmly grasp the future. If your heart is constantly filled with the fear of letting go of the familiar and that which you control, then how will you be able to receive the new blessings that the Lord has in store for you? Imagine both of your hands were filled with groceries and the Lord had a $100,000 in twenty-dollar bills to give you. How much of that money would you be able to grasp if you did not want to let go of the groceries?

Let's take a moment to examine the situation. It's quite easy to choose to let go of two arms full of groceries for a $100K of cash because one can easily see that the cash has more value than the groceries. Or does it? A bag of groceries often contains bread, juice, milk, hygienic supplies and perhaps something to cook.

However, an emotional bag of groceries often includes items that through years of practice have become intertwined in our character. This makes them more difficult to readily give up even if we know it is best to let go of them. Some of these items may be bitterness, resentment, hurt, fear, rage, anger and the lack of forgiveness. Unforgiveness is probably the most harmful parcel in this bag of emotional groceries.

As my friend Dr. Dick Tibbits wrote in his book, *Forgive to Live*, the lack of forgiveness is the constant mental replay of the initial hurt over and over. This further empowers the person who caused your hurt. In most cases, this person is not the least bit affected by your restricted ability to live, love and laugh. You may be able to take courage in the fact that the offending person may not even be aware that the act they committed has caused you the pain you are feeling. The most ironic fact about our lack of forgiveness is that the very reason for Jesus dying on the cross is the forgiveness of our sins.

The situation is clear. Jesus wants to give you a gift of greater value than that you are holding. Letting go is critical if not crucial to your growth in Christ and your quest for purpose. As you can see, there is a true struggle in being "free from to being free for". Your perspective here should be that change is simply movement into my next phase of development. Sometimes struggle is necessary to formulate the character that is needed to thrive within that next phase.

Don't be afraid of failure

Henry Ford said, "Failure is the opportunity to begin again more intelligently". One of my favorite writers, Napoleon Hill says, "The strongest oak tree of the forest is not the one that is protected from the storm and hidden from the sun. It's the one that stands in the open where it is compelled to struggle for its existence against the winds and rains and the scorching sun". Another great quote is one brought to prominence by author Bill Allin, who wrote," The road to success leads through failure".

Many of us are intimidated by the fact God would actually uses us for any task, let alone an awesome task like the one we are sensing deep in our existence. Think of Moses who spent the first 40 years of his life thinking he was somebody, the next 40 years realizing he was nobody and his last 40 years realizing what God can do with a no-body. Imagine if Moses feared Pharaoh more than God when God told him what to tell Pharaoh. Who then, would God have used to free the Jews if Moses ran off to the desert in fear of failure? What would life be like in this country for persons of color if Dr. Martin Luther King, Jr. suddenly developed a fear of failure and fled to Europe with his family?

What will the future hold for your life and the lives you touch if you took your life this instant because the stress of life was too much to handle? This is what we do each time we fail to heed the directional signs the Holy Spirit sends us to step out on faith. We actually kill our chances of growing toward purpose and abort all the possibilities of touching the lives the Lord has lined up in our path for residual blessings.

"Life is not destiny's finale or the finals in the Olympics, surely life must be lived carefully and with sound judgment to avoid tragedy, but the fear of failure should not be its driving force".
Getting over the fear of failure is not a process. I'm not saying that we would strive for failure or mediocrity; I am simply saying that success is a process and sometimes that process takes you down a street called failure.

Most of the top executives in Corporate America got there and can affectively lead there because of what they have learned from their failures. They can affectively lead people because they have learned what it was like to fail people.

God allows failure to also give us a chance to behold His salvation. When Jesus healed the Blind man, he did it in three steps. He could have simply laid hands on Him or speak to him and it would have been done. Jesus spit on the ground and made a paste with is sputum. Then He rubbed in onto the man's eyelids. He asked the man to reveal what he saw. The man rubbed his eyes and said I see men as trees. Jesus repeated the same action and then the man saw clearly. Jesus did it twice. Did He do so because He failed the first time? The answer is no. What appears to be failure to us is only an added stage to Christ. You see, delays can come for three reasons:

1. Our faith or lack thereof
2. It's not our season
3. To illustrate the awesome power of God at work

Do you remember the story of Moses parting the Red Sea? Why didn't God just simply speed up the process like cutting through a block of cheese with a laser? It took time for the Red Sea to part because God had to displace tens of millions of gallons of water. He allowed it to take enough time so that the children of Israel can marvel and ponder the power of God at work. Most miracles that He allows cannot be viewed from behind the scenes because their nature is a supernatural one. This miracle they can see happening as it is taking place spiritually and naturally.

You can either wrap your mind around the concept or not. These are some of the reasons we use for not being able to do so:

1. Taking ourselves too seriously.
2. Being too concerned of what others think of us.
3. Seeing failure as a wall and not a path.
4. Seeing life as a competition between us and them.
5. Failure means that I will have to start over again.

You philosophers can probably come up with about at least 20 others. The fact is, overcoming failure is a survival technique like teaching a toddler to swim. There is no judgment on technique as long as the child can save themselves. In my estimation, most of us get very uptight about failure for many reasons, but they all pale in comparison from the reward one receives when you finally get it right for yourself.

Don't be afraid of your mortality

I know death is a morbid thought that many would rather not discuss under any circumstances. It reeks of finality and hopelessness. It has no recollection, no knowledge, no vantage point nor does it have any feeling. From the time that we understand what it is as a child, it has already brought much pain and anguish to those we love.

Death has quickly become our mortal enemy. The bible refers to death as separation from God, but it also says that to be absent from the flesh is to be present with God (2 Cor 5:6-8). Our apprehension with death is simply because we cannot have a discussion with it as we can with someone in a hospital bed. It shows neither bias nor prejudice. It is neither logical nor irrational.

It just doesn't make sense and it always plays strictly by its own rules. Deaths biggest mystery is that those who visit death become permanent residents and never send any post cards, pictures or any videos. We have concerns that death is only a passage way that leads to two distinctly different destinations, heaven and hell. Unlike U-tube and Google, we cannot do a quick search on either location and find interviews or sound bites. One key way to become more knowledgeable about death is to read what death was intended for in the book of Revelations. The other way to become more comfortable with death is to get intimately acquainted with God, who is the only competent authority on the subject.

Spending time with God while you work, love, laugh, cry, yell, scream and live will give you a better understanding of His mysteries and His heart. In fact, spending time with God will reveal things to you that are not in the bible. *Death is a definitive passage way for your spirit to travel back to eternity where it was created. Our body was created in time and our souls were created by God in eternity. We tend to fear the ways in which this passage way is approached.*

Some transition through death after saying good-bye to their loved ones by their side as they peacefully fall asleep; others transition painfully and violently without warning or closure with loved ones.

Many of us have dreaded memories of loved ones dying of an illness that slowly denies them of life's basic dignity. Either way we look at it; this is a subject we would rather skip. God taught me that purpose is directly tied to its completion. Simply put, there is an aspect of death you must embrace before you reach your knowledge of purpose.

This mindset is a process and a journey in and of itself. When I came to the knowledge of this necessary passage to our eternity, I started thinking of it almost every day. Before you pass judgment on me as some ideologue on death, please take a moment to follow what I am saying.

Shortly before the birth of my first son, Satan started to tell me that I would never live to see his birth. This was my second marriage and I never shared this thought with my wife, out of fear; I did not want to confess this thought. On Thursday, May 28th, 1998 at 12:46 p.m., my son, Christian David, was born. I fell to my knees with tears of joy and gratitude for his birth and life.

He was born by C-section and he did not open his eyes for several hours. When he did open his eyes while in my arms in the nursery, I cried a second time with gratitude that God allowed me to live and see my son face to face. Knowing the lie that Satan told me, I was even more grateful for my life at his birth. Getting to finally meet this child who had prayed so much for was such a blessing.

Ever since then, like most parents, my life had new meaning. I literally lived each day as though it were my last. By that I mean I never took any time with him or my wife for granted. I worked hard and served the Lord in any way I could. Shortly before the birth of my second son, Aaron, the enemy told me the same thing again.

He said I will kill you in your sleep before the birth of your second son and they both will forget your memory before they grow up. On December, 14th, 2000 at 8:26 a.m., my son, Aaron Alexander, was born and I was there to hold him and thank God for both of us *being there.*

Both pregnancies were high risk for my wife and threatened both her and our sons' lives. ***I then started to weep not only for my gratitude for life but for the sorrow I felt for all the parents who did not have this opportunity to see the birth of their child.*** This was the case of my mother's father and many soldiers who fight courageously on distant shores to ensure the freedoms we take for granted every day.

God showed himself to be mighty and faithful. There has not been one day since that I have not thought of my mortality. I spend each day loving and preparing my sons for the day that I make that transition to eternity. I teach them good communication skills and to add to life, not just take away. I illustrate examples of how not to be judgmental and selfish, but rather to be empathetic and to share.

I make sure they understand that I am their father and not their peer so they respect my words and admonishment without question when necessary, yet they are still able to utter phrases like "We wish you were our age so we could play with you all the time 'cause you're so much fun". That always chokes me up when I hear it. I see the return for the hard work when they both see me hard at work outside or sitting for hours at the computer and come to me with a tall cold glass of water to refresh myself.

This tells me that they will make the time to observe how to serve their God and how to nurture and serve their future wives, their family and mankind. I am truly honored and consider it a privilege to father Christian and Aaron Cort. As I write these words, my prayer is that you are able to feel and illustrate the same sentiment about your children as well.

You're probably thinking that I'm overindulgent in my children and what does that have to do with helping me cope with my mortality? The fact is I'm a better person for it because I am healing my own wounds from my childhood. I am sewing good seed back into life by creating character in my sons that God can use without having to take precious time to break them down and start over again. These young men will enter adulthood with God's grace ready to serve and lead. ***They have become my most profound teachers because the Lord has my undivided attention through them.***

God tends to deal with us in story and mirrored form. During His ministry on earth, He spoke in parables (stories) and allowed time to mirror our lives as the meaning in those stories unfurled. We see children as a clean canvas for us to create what we want them to be, the story. But they are also cameras with microphones that capture the true honesty of what we are into their spirit and they will play the tape back at the most profound times. These playbacks tell the truth of what we are and what we've created, which either will bring us outward embarrassment and inner shame or pride and confidence.

Now that I am more mature and centered firmly in my knowledge of the Lord, I understand that He used these thoughts of mortality to tightly knit my mind and His spirit into the tapestry He calls my purpose. When you think that your days are numbered you tend to waste less time and use your days with more thought, planning, silence and purpose.

As you get closer to realizing and flourishing in what that purpose is, you would have spent so much time with God in instruction, that death and dying does not cause you the anxiety it previously did. You have now become intimate with the people, activities and fears that have kept you off balance during your entire existence. You will find the selfishness that you once had about missing out on life after death and how your family and friends will live on are exchanged with "Look at what a wonderful life God and I have lived during this time He's given me here. I have taken on so many challenges with Him by my side, I can now take on anything".

Your mortality challenge may be with a sick parent or with sickness yourself. It may be with a job, a friend or even the person who torments your life most. God is well capable of using that scenario to acquaint you with your mortality clock which may just end up being a long life filled with purpose.

THE SCIENCE OF CHANGE

We are all born with behavioral instincts such as a baby's ability to suck and swallow or to pull our finger back if it gets too close to a flame. As captured in their book, *Core Concepts in Cultural Anthropology*, Emily A. Schultz and Robert H. Lavenda, 1987 said human beings are more dependent on learning for survival than other species. We have no instincts that automatically protect us and find us food and shelter, for example."

As humans, we are taught what to fear and what to respect. If you come from a family that has lost many adults to drowning accidents because none of them can swim, then as a child you will be taught that water is a dangerous thing and that you should stay away from bodies of water at all costs. Unless someone takes the time or you choose to take the initiative to conquer this fear, this ignorance and this tradition, you will remain at that level of consciousness for the rest of your life. The same applies with the fear of all dogs, cats and heights.

The desire to learn and grow intellectually and spiritually can literally change your life and destiny. You will hear this several times throughout this book. Through knowledge we can actually override genetically programmed instincts like our heart rate, breathing, blood pressure, body temperature and even our bleeding patterns.

Think of it, if you perceive that you are in danger, you brain will immediately raise your blood pressure, heart rate and adrenaline levels. That is why master martial artists, experts in meditation and Yogis are able to control these factors upon demand; so you can too. If this is possible on such a high personal developmental level, don't you think you can choose to change not being easily offended or not to complain so much?

If you truly want to change the way your mind and your history have been ruling your life, there is enough scientific data that supports how allowing a higher power to aid your deficient knowledge base can push you to do more toward making a positive change in your life. In his book *The Biology of Belief,* Dr. Lipton shares a story about a student attending Sheffield University in the U.K. who has an IQ of 126. According the American Psychological Association (APA) 50% of Americans have an IQ of 90-109. An IQ of 120-129 is considered superior.

What makes this student so unusual besides the fact that he is so intelligent is the fact that he is missing most of the brain tissue in his cranium. British neurologist Dr. John Lorber specifically points out in a 1980 article in Science "Is your Brain Really Necessary?", that the size of your brain is the most important consideration for human intelligence. Although individuals can

93

live a normal life with less cerebral cortex, it is unusual for them to be so intelligent.

This further supports the understanding that with knowledge of a higher power, one can truly achieve anything they truly want to intellectually. As we have all seen in the media lately, this applies to physical and emotional challenges too.

Generational curses can stop in the generation of the man or woman that chooses to no longer be controlled by what ignorance, fear and tradition dictate. My sister, you are not an accident nor are you intended to be a misfit. God has formed you in His very image. Although we were born in sin and shaped in its iniquity, we can change.

This scientific data shows that we can change even if we want to without knowing Christ; that makes you a conqueror. Changing while you know Christ makes you more than a conqueror. Now you have the power to know what to speak to your cells so that they behave consistently.

Did you know that cancer cells thrive in acidic environments? The negative thoughts that drive some of us create an acidic environment in our bodies. Cancer cells grow best in these environments. Did you know that cancer cells live in our bodies on a daily basis? It's true. We live with cancer every day even if you are the healthiest triathlete. The fact is that the cancer cells are kept at bay by our healthy cells which outnumber the cancer cells. Our healthy cells thrive in a highly oxygenated environment which is created by avoiding excessive sweets and eating living foods like fresh fruits and vegetables.

Positive thinking, laughter and spirituality or something to look forward to helps foster this life giving environment. This oxygenated environment is toxic to cancer cells and keeps them in limited numbers. The moment you decide to eliminate negativity from your thought life, you literally begin to speak life to your body on the cellular level which is essentially where life begins and ends. Obedience means changing one's life when it is not in harmony with the scriptures.

Once again, the prevailing purpose of this book is to help you to try a different approach to being single. You must first give THE man, Jesus Christ what He wants of you before you can expect Him to give you the man you want. God is a jealous God. He will not have any other gods before Him. If your life is postured a certain way with the sole motive of getting a man, then you will find yourself always coming up short. *Your destiny is a not a matter of chance but a matter of choice. Change your mind, change your destiny.* Dating websites won't tell you that.

CHAPTER FIVE

TAKING CARE OF BUSINESS

When you take an inward journey, you will not only find the wreckage, you will also find the buried treasure.

MIRROR, MIRROR

*A*s Christian adults we tend to devote more time on how we want to be perceived rather than how we truly are. We want to be viewed as respectable, intelligent and good Christians. We all know we may not necessarily be those things but we certainly want to be viewed that way. For the mere reason that girdles, hair coloring, make-up, false eye lashes, false hair, weaves, acrylic nails, lip plumping make-up, under garments that enhance; colors and garments that make us look taller, thinner, fuller and finally, younger.

Certainly there is nothing wrong with us wanting to enhance what we have or simply wanting to feel more confident in an area of our lives. But when these augmentations or their intent permeate our character then "Houston we have a problem." It's one thing to want to look better than your DNA planned or your choices yielded but entirely another when you pretend to be something that you are not. The words for that are liar, hypocrite, philanderer, deceitful, conniving and oh yes, a fake. Sometimes we quickly use these words to describe other people yet we completely overlook the biggest offender, US.

Mirrors, cameras and video recorders have the uncanny ability of always being right. They capture the fact without any prejudice at all. Unlike us these devices don't rationalize as a coping mechanism for truth the way we do. Truth merits no reward, nor does it dignify a response. Truth is supreme, therefore absolute."

When you learn to embrace the fact that first, you may not appear how you perceive yourself then that is the beginning of growth. Everyone needs a coping mechanism at some point for any reason. But when you live this coping mechanism, then you are living a lie to yourself and eventually you will pay in one way or another for that lie.

If you one day intend on marrying a spirit filled believer who is as into you as you are into yourself then he will notice your lie and confront you with it. No one can live a lie 24/7 despite how w4ell or long you have been doing it. (numbers 32:23) *"...and you may be sure that your sin will find you out."* (John 8:32), *"Then you will know the truth, and the truth will set you free."* (2 Corinthians 3:17), *"Now the Lord is the Spirit, and where the Spirit of the Lord is, there is freedom."*

Not applicable you say? Here's my point, when you hold anything in your spirit that resembles a willful fabrication then you are not fully engaging the power or the intimacy of the Holy Spirit to release you. Your spirit desires to be free from burdens, the same way that your soul is yearning to leave your body and return back home to the immediate presence of the Lord. The mate the Lord blesses you with will detect the restlessness in your soul whether you admit it or not. We may be able to lie but our subconscious mind and our spirit cannot.

At the writing of this book I am 43 years of age and I am in my third marriage. One can easily sit on the seat of judgment and say how can you have three failed marriages and be saved? My answer is, very easily. If you love the Lord but have not yet come full circle with you honesty with self then you can make bad personal decisions in all areas of your life and still go to heaven. There are married people who fantasize about someone else for a fleeting moment.

They are quick to criticize someone for divorcing their spouse for departing from their faith and jeopardizing the walk of the believer; but they will not admit to the fact that they committed adultery in their mind (Matthew 5:28), *"But I tell you that anyone who looks at a woman lustfully has already committed adultery with her in his heart".* This applies to women too and adultery is also grounds for their spouse to divorce them.

At some point even after the counseling had exonerated me from blame for divorcing two women, I had to come clean and realize that it was all my fault because I proposed marriage in the first place and I sought divorce. So this begs the question of what portion of the blame for the breakdown of the marriages does the Lord place on me? The answer is most of it. Why? Because I am the man and I own up to the fact that I am a man. A real man.

In the Garden of Eden Adam failed God because he was responsible for keeping God's rule relative to safeguarding the forbidden fruit. It may have been one thing if he was about a mile away when Eve was tempted but he was there and allowed it to happen.

The failures in those marriages happened under my watch and that is a fact. I can't honestly say that I fasted for my marriage as often as I should have. I can't say that I laid before the Lord for hours on end as I should have. Surely I did fast and surely I did seek the face of God privately and laboriously.

But the fact remains that I was the one that made up my mind to be fed up with the situation and end the marriages. This is no small admission and it was not an admission that I would have received from a counselor as they looked down their long sanctimonious nose in judgment of me. I was able to make this personal confession to myself after a close and long look at my behaviors and choices.

My mirror, mirror experience came as a result me of desperately wanting to be transparent and free of my own pride and arrogance issues. I wanted Him to empty me out of the residue of flesh and fill me up with Him. I like to use the example of the clean glass and the dirty glass. (2 Timothy 2:20-22) *In a large house there are articles not only of gold and silver, but also of wood and clay; some are for noble purposes and some for ignoble. If a man cleanses himself from the latter, he will be an instrument for noble purposes, made holy, useful to the Master and prepared to do any good work.* When you go to the cupboard to get a clean glass to serve a guest you look at the glass to ensure it is clean and spot free.

If you look into the glass and see stains and residue from what was in there last, you will use another glass instead. The unclean glass will have to be washed out in order to be used. This is the same basic premise with the Lord. If you are unwilling to empty yourself out and allow Him to clean out the entire residue then He will not be able to use you for service to His Kingdom.

You have to make the determination that you want to be a vessel of honor. Part of this self-analysis comes from a mirror, mirror discussion with self. This isn't the tough kind of discussion most people want to have with anyone, except if you have an accountability partner. So in order to see if you truly appear how you perceive yourself you must first be honest willing to admit that there is something that needs to be exposed and/or dealt with.

You can ask the Lord's help in doing so very simply by saying this prayer with me. "*Lord, I know that there are some desires and tendencies that I possess that are offensive to you. Lord please take these issues from me. Lord, in fact please take my desire to repeat these tendencies. Remove the taste from my spirit for these tendencies so that I may be a vessel of honor for your service. Lord, in place of these desires please fill the holes and empty spaces with more of a desire to please you and serve you. In Jesus name. Amen!*"

See how simple that was. No one heard you, so you don't have to explain anything or fear being judged by anyone.

GOOD HABITS, BAD HABITS

During our time as single people we see this as an opportunity to be free and uninhibited. That can be a good and a bad thing. The good thing is you can walk around your home in your underwear or totally nude if you choose to. The bad part is, you can get into bad habits that are bad to break when you meet someone new. Take for instance making your bed.

You've probably heard the old saying about always wearing clean underwear because if you get into an accident the emergency care workers will see that you have dirty underwear and you'll be embarrassed. I know that may be a bit far-fetched for some, but it is really more of the understanding of self-pride than anything else. After all why would you want to wear dirty underwear anyway unless you are too lazy to wash your clothes in a timely manner; that's another point we'll get to later.

Keeping a clean home is a direct reflection on you regardless of how free and uninhibited you want to be. The habits you allow yourself to become steeped in as a single person will become extremely difficult to break when you meet Mr. Right. Try taking a look at your habits and housekeeping regimen. On any given day you should be able to have unexpected company over to your home and allow them to use your bathroom with the confidence of knowing both are clean. Other habits to closely examine are how you stock your pantry and how you organize your bills and finances.

Keeping note of your bill payments and checking account information on backs of envelopes and scrap paper is not a good sign of someone who is organized. Believe it or not those are some of the habits that can cause raise red flags to a man who prides himself on being neat and being financially stable.

Another thing that single people don't take not of until they get called on it is how you keep your bedroom and your closet. If your bedroom and your closet at this very moment looks like you were robbed by someone looking for the needle in the hay stack, then maybe you should consider cleaning things up a bit.

No man wants a woman who is more of a mess than he is. To be quite honest your walk with God is reflected in the way you look, the way you carry yourself and the way you keep your home. Try to get into the habit of making your bed before you leave the house and putting away your clothes when you take them off.

I understand leaving your dry cleaned clothes on a hanger to air out before putting them back in the closet but they should be put away by the next morning. Put away your under garments and feminine products in their proper place so that you don't have to scramble when you hear your door bell ring or that your girlfriend or boyfriend is nearby and they need to use your bathroom.

I've heard some women who are working hard and long hours who say that they don't have the time and I know women who say they don't have the means to wash their clothes regularly. I answer I have for both scenarios is to plan and improvise.

If you work long hours, plan ahead to cook your meals, do your laundry and spend 10 minutes straightening up. If money is tight you can still improvise. When I was a broke 20 year old bachelor, I use to fill the tub with cool water and use dishwashing liquid to wash the clothes I needed to get me through the week until I either got paid or carped up enough money to get to the Laundromat.

Being single and complete is not really a time to be filled with excuses and mediocrity, it's about being ready on all fronts for the Lord and being in position spiritually and natural for getting found by Mr. Right.

The word budget for a single person of any demographical group is the real "B" word and should be avoided at all times. Living on a budget will discipline you to leave within your means as a married person. Poor money habits are the cause of almost 50% of failed marriages according to Bureau of Labor Statistics and the 2000 U.S. Census and virtually every competent survey; poor financial management and communication is within the top five reasons for divorce today. No we all can understand loss of employment and under-employment causing hard times but over spending on a consistent basis is not acceptable.

If your spending is out of control, it may be a good idea to talk to a financial counselor so that you can establish better spending habits. In terms of work, you should realize that your attitude toward your work even if you feel like you are in a dead end job and the anti-Christ is your boss, should be a reflection of your service to the Lord. (Colossians 3:22) *Slaves, obey your earthly masters in everything; and do it, not only when their eye is on you and to win their favor, but with sincerity of heart and reverence for the Lord*

Although we are not slaves, the term is applicable to your vocation or work. Paul is saying that your attitude toward our work is a form of worship because it is a reflection of your relationship with the Lord. Don't just get to work barley on time and try to leave five minutes early.

Don't be a clock watcher and do the bare minimum that is required of you. This is a poor witness to those who know that you are a Christian and it makes you look bad to the Father who you will ask for another job if you were to lose this one. Try to make your walk with God permeate all areas of your life so that you will never be called a hypocrite.

MASTER THE EXCHANGE

The laws of reciprocity are often misunderstood as only the give and take mantra between people. The same applies in Quantum Physics and Newtonian studies. Biomedical scientists clearly state when there is a constant our flow or feed forward without receiving or feedback, it creates a vacuum or a void that brings imbalance.

If a cell cannot withstand the pressure exerted against its membrane then it will implode on itself. If you suck all the air out of an aluminum can then it will crush like a Dixie cup. The bible captures the same principle of give and take in (Luke 6:38) *Give, and it will be given to you. A good measure, pressed down, shaken together and running over, will be poured into your lap. For with the measure you use, it will be measured to you."*

Give and take is a wonderful concept as long as you're not the only one giving. Life certainly has its share of takers. Many of us feel that we got our share and someone else's share as well. When folks see that you have a giving heart and that you are also trusting; it seems to send out a secret hormone that only leeches can detect. As a single woman

I'm sure that life has placed you on the imbalanced side of reciprocity, which is enough to taint your view of giving. There is no promise written anywhere in any religion of philosophical mantra that says life is supposed to be fair and people are supposed to treat you right.

In fact religion and virtually all of the 40 plus religions in the world teach their members how to manage you in spite of the evil intended world around us. As referenced in chapter four; you may not be able to control the actions of those around you but you can certainly control their effect on you. By allowing the selfish and arrogant ways of men and anyone for that matter to change your loving and giving nature means that evil prevailed over good. Don't let people and their selfish ways rent space in your head; the real estate between your ears is too expensive to lease it out and in some cases give it away.

Just because Oscar, Bill, Robert and every man you have ever been involved with took more from you than they have given doesn't mean that all men are that way. It also doesn't mean that you shouldn't be the way that you are.

One of the biggest problems that Jesus has with the church is that we are too sensitive and too inconsistent. As soon as someone does us wrong we want to retreat and become Mr. Hyde and morph into this secretive and ugly existence. If you determine to change and become a selfish introvert, don't do it because the world did you bad. Do it because you secretly want to. Jesus doesn't cry tears because someone lied to you or on you.

He doesn't get moved because someone took something from you or didn't pay you back the loan you were promised of getting back. He especially isn't moved by the fact that people keep misunderstanding you and talk about you behind your back. Remember my friend, they did it Him too. This world is never to accept you and love the ground you walk on. If you claim to be living anything for Jesus at all you may as well understand that persecution is the rent you pay for claiming the name of Jesus. We are labeled in Christ as a peculiar people passing through this place on our way home someday (1 Peter 2:9) KJV *"But ye [are] a chosen generation, a royal priesthood, an holy nation, a peculiar people; that ye should shew forth the praises of him who hath called you out of darkness into his marvelous light."*

Jesus is never impressed by your academic prowess or even what wonderful professional and economic success you have gleaned from the opportunities He has afforded you. Jesus is only moved with the attitude in which you handle crisis and storms.

Remember, any Good thing that you have ever been given or have gained access to is a direct result of God's grace and mercy upon your life and nothing more. So don't get it twisted by believing that you actually deserve anything that you have. Your expression of love to God is how you represent Him to everyone at any given time. (Matthew 25:40) *The King will reply, 'I tell you the truth, whatever you did for one of the least of these brothers of mine, you did for me.'*

Whatever you are lacking in your life is a direct result of what you are not sowing. If you want people to show you appreciation and gratitude you must first show it. If you want to be shown love and affection, you must first be affectionate and loving toward others. How can someone be loving toward you unless you are first loveable. If you walk around all day like you're sucking on lemons, there is no possible way that anyone would be motivated to give you the love you are desperately in search of. The universal principles of reciprocity command that you have to give out before you can receive. There is no possible way that you can give with love continually and not have it come back to you. You must sow in the area that you want to reap.

This is a principle that has been followed for thousands of years. Do you really think that it would change for the mere fact that you are now walking the earth? As mentioned in chapter one, my desire is to not offend you. But I care about your growth and spiritual enough to be absolutely honest with you.

I don't know you, so you know this can't be personal. In order to have a radical change you must be radical in your motive and radical in your approach. If you want oranges you can't plant tomato seeds. If you want cabbage you can't sow apple seeds. If you want love and kindness you must first sow in that area. Even if it is not readily returned; you must also understand that the harvest can only come in its season.

If you plant a seed, it does not begin to bear fruit right away. Depending on the kind of plant it may take years for it to produce anything. But if you stop nurturing it and feeding it according to its needs then it will die because you have given up on it and you will never get to see the fruits of your labor.

God also wants to observe your motive for doing what you do. If you want to sow just so you can get, then you have not proven that you can take care of it when you are blessed with it. Lots of folks want a dog because they see how cute it is as a puppy. But there is a lot of work involved in raising a dog from a puppy. A lot of that work requires patience and commitment. This commitment comes with discipline and maturity not just because the dog is cute. Many of us want love or power because of the way it makes us feel.

What we don't want is the work we must put in in order to grow and cultivate it. We just see for the moment the puppy or the love or the power when someone else possesses it. That is just the tip of the ice berg or the plant above the surface. What you don't see is the dirt and the root system that is sustaining the plant. That root system took years to cultivate from feeding, pruning, and watering.

You have to ward off the bugs and parasites as well as cover it from the cold and shield it from too much sun when needed. You don't see that part. When you see the beautiful dog and want to pet it. You don't hear about the shoes that he ruined and the carpet and furniture that was destroyed.

All you are seeing is the fact that he is cute and cuddly. After he ruins your favorite pocket book or $300 suede sling backs, he's not so cuddly anymore. Then what? Do you take him to the pound and have him put to sleep? Or do you put in the time and train him the way you want him to be.

That is what sowing is all about. It is about commitment. God wants to see your commitment. If your blessing or harvest is a child, how are you raising her? Is she filled with the resentment of your impatience and bitterness because she didn't give you what you wanted when you wanted it? If you are a single parent then this should resonate with you clearly. Your commitment is not measured by the time you put in until it is no longer convenient or fun. It is measured by the attitude and the consistency by which you do a thing until it is complete.

So if you find that you are still waiting, check your attitude and your spiritual calendar. It may not be your time or your season.

The bigger the anticipated harvest, the more time needs to be spent sowing. Once again, if you are lacking in an area you have to first sow in that area to reap the harvest for such. God is a God of reasoning and intellect.

He established the Universe of 150 billion galaxies against a back drop of scientific principles that man has yet to scratch the surface of fathoming. With that understanding do you not think that He also established how we should govern our lives in the natural and spiritual realm?

"Rejoice with those who rejoice, mourn with those who mourn" (Romans 12:15). *"Give and it shall be given onto you." For God so loved the world that He GAVE"*. If someone accomplishes something then be genuinely glad for them like it were happening for you. When in a conversation with someone who is bragging about their children or a family member, don't just pause in anticipation while giving the obligatory nod and smile and waiting your turn of doing the same. Listen with general interest as though this is someone who has good news to share with you and that Jesus is standing there listening, because He truly is. Most people today are only interested of hearing themselves talk and brag about what they have and what they do. *"Be the change you want the world to become"*. That quote was attributed to Ghandi who believed that you must first illustrate what you want to see in the world around you.

So think back to the people you have miss-treated indirectly or as a direct result of something you were going through or because of a certain status God allowed you to achieve and enjoy, just remember that you did the same thing to Jesus. Continue to give I the name of Jesus, not blindly and without sound judgment but without prejudice and guile.

The person you bless may be the one to introduce you to the man that has almost given up on kind and giving people. Your obedience may be the catalyst that brings your destiny to his. I'm sure you have seen the movie or two with the same story line. Always be compassionate and treat people the way you would want your child or your loved one to be treated. Remember that you are a servant that plays to only one Master not the accolades of man.

Mankind is so fickle that he or she may praise you today and curse you tomorrow. I would like to share an excerpt from my Snack Food for the Soul devotional that I send out weekly. This one-minute inspirational read is sent out every Monday morning at midnight. You can sign up for this to come directly to your e-mail inbox at www.thepowerofperspective.net. This excerpt is called:

AN AUDIENCE OF ONE

As a former radio and television personality, the Lord has blessed me with many rich experiences that I certainly did not deserve. Some of those experiences involved speaking to millions of people through a microphone or a TV camera. Some of the most rewarding opportunities came while speaking and ministering to thousands of people on the stage of some of the most recognizable venues in New York City.

Fewer earthly accolades can compare to the roar and the applause coming from the seats of Radio City Music Hall, Madison Square Garden, Carnegie Hall, Lincoln Center and the Apollo Theater just to name a few. Whether I was introducing George Benson, Luis Palau or receiving fan mail for a job well done; it all gave me a feeling of love, accomplishment and appreciation.

So, did I mention all of this to impress you about my past? The answer is no. In fact the preceding words were possibly the most difficult to write in all the devotionals I've ever shared.

My expertise is not in talking about my victories; my gift and passion lies in telling the stories of my failures and how to keep others from making the same.

During those years of being a recognizable figure, I never lost sight of the fact that God had placed good people in my path that saw something in me worth giving opportunity to. As a gesture of gratitude and humility I took great pride in treating everyone I met with the highest level of respect and courtesy. The critical mistake I made in those youthful years was that I didn't treat the Lord with the same level of respect and courtesy. I'm sure you've heard the quote that "There is a thin line between love and hate." Life and great pain has taught me that there is a gulf that separates loving God and being intimate with Him.

I walked away from all those accomplishments and two failed marriages to finally understand what pure intimacy with the Holy Spirit truly is. I spent the most productive years of my life working full time, putting myself through under-grad and graduate school while trying my best to please people more than God.

I knew the voice of my theology professor, my boss, my many mentors and my wife more than I knew the voice of God. Everyone knew what was best for me except me. Surely I was saved and filled with the Holy Spirit but I wrestled almost daily between what I knew to be right versus what would make me accepted by man. The bible calls that disobedience.

Most of us go the extra mile more for people than we do for Christ. When you take Christ into your confidence and He becomes your advisor, counselor, mediator and best friend; you will find Truth. Truth Merits no reward, nor does it dignify any response. Truth, like God, is sovereign and therefore absolute. Once we get use to living in, with and for the sake of Truth, we will never be forsaken. Jesus said, He is the way, the truth and the life.

When we ignore the audience of God, He sees this as driving in a car with someone you say you passionately love. While you're driving you come to a stop light, then scream out and burst into tears. At the next stop sign you break out in hysterical laughter, then at the left turn, you start to yell in rage and anger. With each outburst of emotion you completely ignore Him as though He wasn't even there.

Instead of quieting our soul and emotions to convey our smiles and pains to Him, we leave Him out in the cold, so to speak. In reality He wants to reside within us. How can we be in such close proximity to the Spirit of God yet remaining unchanged?

We have become so accustomed to seeking outside carnal remedies for our spiritual ills.
By performing to an audience of one in Christ Jesus, we will never feel alone or have our secrets betrayed, because He can keep a secret (Hebrews 13:5)
"...never will I leave you, never will I forsake you."

By performing to an audience of one in the Lord, we never need to over compensate for not feeling loved because (Jeremiah 31:3) "... I will love you with an everlasting love..." When you take your secret sins and shameful thoughts to the Lord for healing and restoration, He said in His word (1 John 1:9) "If we confess our sins, He is faithful and just and will forgive us our sins and purify us from all unrighteousness."

The Lord even goes as far to teach in (Psalms 103:12), "As far as the east is from the west, so far has He removed our transgressions from us."When you strive first to please and glorify God in everything you do, you will excel the spirit of mediocrity and dysfunction in your life. Those familiar relations won't even feel comfortable in associating with you any longer. You will naturally flow in a spirit of excellence and favor. It will no longer matter who's watching and taking note of your actions. No concert hall or stadium could quantify the distinguishing tenor of applause from the eternal hands of The audience of one.

CHAPTER SIX

KNOWLEDGE IS POWER

Since our weapons are not carnal, neither should be our thoughts.

TRANFERENCE

*T*he first time I used this phrase was as an adult when I was working at WRKS-FM/ 98.7 KISS-FM in New York. I was the Director of Community Affairs and the host of the most popular Gospel Radio Show in New York. Every community initiative I did had to be big. With the help and confidence of my leadership I was able to promote and produce huge events at Madison Square Garden, Carnegie Hall, Radio City Music Hall and at least a dozen other world renowned venues.

I had another opportunity to make it rain again. This time it was pursuing a dream to partner with a major educational institution to help minority students gain access to the decision makers in this media market.

That vision was called the New York Communications Expo at NYU. It was done three years in a row and serviced over 15,000 students with the opportunity to meet and greet with the industry titans of the time in print, TV, radio and cable. The proceeds from the event went to the Office of AHANA at NYU, which stands for African-Hispanic-Asian-Native-American studies.

The theme of our event was Knowledge is Power. It was the first time I used the phrase as an adult and the audience was 95% women. Which stands to reason that women have always been at the forefront to receive the transference of wisdom that was freely being offered? Once you are empowered with knowledge, you have more options available to you.

SPIRITUAL DAY SPA

If you have ever had a day at the spa you'll know how exhilarating it feels to be pampered from head to toe. Depending on the ingredients of your spa and how intensely they were applied, you can leave feeling as light and refreshed as a cloud floating in midair. Considering the rigors we place on our bodies on a regular basis, a day spa treatment is a nice way of stimulating the senses.

If you have the means and the time; consider a massage and a facial. If you really want to spoil yourself out of love and appreciation for the skin you are in, try a massage, facial and one of those European soaks in minerals and fragrant oils.

If the spa is not your consideration for physical utopia consider visiting a day spa and perusing their menu of treatments to see what suits your fancy. Have you ever considered doing the same for your spirit? Many in the church body think the best way of treating your spirit to any kind of exhilaration is by simply having quiet time. That assumption would be correct if your life was complete utter chaos every day.

But if you want to give your soul more, there is more, much more. I'm going to share something with you that you won't hear in many churches. In this age of brevity and packaging, most

Pastors don't have the time and luxury to teach in depth on any subject at all. So the spiritual diet of most evangelical churches is not beyond the nutritional depth of a hot pocket, a melted cheese sandwich or a selection from the dollar menu of your favorite fast food franchise. The soul of America is starving for in depth knowledge of the word and intimacy with the Spirit of Christ.

I bet you are wondering where I am going with this. You see if you have ever been intimate with any man that you are no longer in a relationship with, then you should know that you are now carrying around the spirit of every woman he has ever slept with. This includes the spirit of every man she has ever slept with.

This further includes the sexual behavior of every homosexual relationship their previous partner and their network of lovers have ever been with, and so on and so on. This is why AIDS and other STD's are so common nowadays. You never just have sex with one person. That is why it is so important to remain abstinent until married. But of course no one does that anymore because it is considered so old school and archaic.

Think about it, haven't you ever found yourself dealing with mental and physical issues that are completely out of your familiar? It could be that you caught something that has been in someone else's family for generations. What's even scarier is that some of these transferred demons can remain dormant in you for years and years and jump onto your children. Then all of a sudden your child's spouse in 20 plus years is dealing with something that no one in your family has ever dealt with before. Yes, it is possible to catch more than a cold or an STD in your next sexual encounter. Now you see that there are more issues at play in your failed relationships than just what you've been conditioned to believe.

The enemy works best in anonymity just like vampires in the old Hollywood science fiction movies. The police would happen on a scene filled with dead bodies with puncture wounds to the neck and they would scratch their heads in wonderment. The enemy operates the same way. In some ways we give him too much power and in other ways we fail to think he exists at all.

Unless you are blessed to be a member of a church that teaches the word and spiritual awareness, you are basically suffering from spiritual malnourishment. God bless the pastors who are in this position, they are trying to do the best with what they have got.

Unfortunately for most of them, they too wish they could be fed and ministered to on a consistent basis the way they wish they had the expertise or the grace to teach. With that being said, here is what I want to share. Remember my brief conversation with you on generational curses in chapter four? Well here is the second part of how to rid your spirit of all its excess baggage by way of secret sin, lusts, addictions, moodiness and the demons that remain hidden even after you cast out their outward expression.

Jesus punctuates our power to cast out demons in His name (Luke 10:17) *The seventy-two returned with joy and said, "Lord, even the demons submit to us in your name." (*Acts 5:16*), Crowds gathered also from the towns around Jerusalem, bringing their sick and those tormented by evil spirits, and all of them were healed, (*Mark 16:17*) And these signs will accompany those who believe: In my name they will drive out demons; they will speak in new tongues..."*

But as stated before, there is more, much more. If you want to delve into the mysterious world of the spiritual there is always more to quench your curiosity while satisfying you soul. After 17 plus years in the deliverance ministry I can tell you first hand that the deliverance you see at the altar of most of our charismatic evangelical church services is powerful and effective but compared to what is really going on with demons in the spiritual realm; what you see is child's play.

Our souls are bombarded by spiritual warfare on a regular basis and if we could see into the spirit realm on a regular basis most of us would run and cower under our beds. Giving your spirit a rest and empowering it to free itself of the demonic baggage that it carries unbeknownst to us involves serious business. This is the kind of stuff you may want to do so that you don't carry the trash that's been chasing you from relationship to relationship into the wonderful marriage you pray the Lord bless you with. As mentioned, the bible is clear about the power that is imbued upon us as children of the most high God, but the bible is also clear that we need to understand to bring our "A" game when getting into spiritual warfare.

(Acts 19:13-16) *Some Jews who went around driving out evil spirits tried to invoke the name of the Lord Jesus over those who were demon-possessed. They would say, "In the name of Jesus, whom Paul preaches, I command you to come out." Seven sons of Sceva, a Jewish chief priest, were doing this. [One day] the evil spirit answered them, "Jesus I know, and I know about Paul, but who are you?" Then the man who had the evil spirit jumped on them and overpowered them all. He gave them such a beating that they ran out of the house naked and bleeding.*

(Mathew 12:43-45), *"When an evil spirit comes out of a man, it goes through arid places seeking rest and does not find it. Then it says, 'I will return to the house I left.' When it arrives, it finds the house unoccupied, swept clean and put in order. Then it goes and takes with it seven other spirits more wicked than itself, and they go in and live there. And the final condition of that man is worse than the first. That is how it will be with this wicked generation."*

117

After 17 years laying on of hands and fasting and prayer, the Lord has shared some insight that is based on an exercise that I will share with you in a moment that will free your soul from unwanted baggage and hidden demons. The key in understanding the enemy and his demons are knowing their weakness in and of themselves and their strength through their influence on us.

I mentioned before that we give the enemy more power than he actually has. That is the fault of Hollywood which by definition of its name is satanic. Holly wood is a magician's stick or a sorcerer's wand that evokes satanic and mystical powers. So basically Hollywood the place, the mecca for movies and false pretense is a wand that waves satanic influences over our nation and the world.

 The enemy of mankind, satan cannot be in more than one place at one time (omni-present), he is not all powerful as in having the ability to cause your death without God's permission (omni-potent) and he cannot read your mind and is not all knowing (omni-scient).

The only similar power he has to omni-scient is the fact that he knows how we think due to our sin nature which comes from him. We were born in sin and shaped in iniquity. Because of this fact, the enemy understands and can predict our lusts, our fears, our addictions and our weaknesses.

So when he tempts us and torments us in the areas that he will never be delivered from then we give him a spiritual promotion to something that he truly isn't. The fact is that satan is a fallen angel. The angels that you have the authority over as mentioned in (Psalms 91:11) are infinitely more powerful than he is and will ever be.

118

In fact you have more power of him than he will ever have over you as well. *"Greater is He that is in you than he that is in the world."* Do you remember that scripture? Well God is saying, because of God's anointing and covering over your life, the enemy cannot have any dominion over you as long as you are in Christ Jesus. With that being said here is the basis for the understanding for the exercise. Every demon that is supposedly cast out isn't always cast out. What most of us see is the outward manifestation or the symptom that is cast out. There are some demons that are satanic strongholds that are the manipulating demon or the sub-jacent demon.

This is the demon that is really in charge of the several we see. This demon can remain hidden for years and years and even outlive us and jump into our closest and youngest living relative until the ideal time to strike. This methodology has been used in the military for thousands of years. Today we call them sleeper cells in this day of terrorism.

These demons lay in wait and go virtually undetected. This demon could have gotten there the day you were born or as a result of a sexual encounter. The deeper the encounter the deeper and stronger the demon has a hold on you. During sex you are not only exchanging physical and emotional pleasure; you are exchanging bodily fluids and spirits.

That is why God intended that sex be reserved for marriage, because if your spirit is as one then you don't run the risk of catching random demons. If your spouse is honest and you both are spirit filled and aware of spiritual warfare then the chances of the hidden demon being exposed are greater.

Yes, they can still be hidden but the chances are less if you are only intimate with one person than having random sex. Remember random sex is having sex with a network of people from your sexual partner's past every time he penetrates you. Do you now begin to see the picture? Are you now beginning to understand how and why all hell has and can break lose in your life?

A few minutes or hours of pure soul trembling pleasure can incarcerate your blood line for generations to come. You will long since have forgotten the orgasm, but you will vividly remember the hell you caused your children and every life they touch.

You will vividly recall the child you caused to be born with developmental problems and other social and physical problems; and you will always wonder if this is as a direct result of your sin. Getting back to the demon that was cast out; when this demon has all his cohorts with him he can hide easily in the shadows. When those cohorts or weaker, demons are cast out then he has to hold on tighter or go into hiding.

This is why some people are delivered from alcoholism and other addictions and sometimes fall back into the addictions at the first cause of temptation or all of a sudden out of the blue. That demon is hiding but not dead. If he sees the opportunity to rise up and cause other lives to crash and burn simultaneously, then he will. Do you remember the Hollywood movie of 1998 starring Denzel Washington and John Goodman, called *Fallen*? The demon that was depicted always sung a song called *Time is on my side*. The fact is once again, that Hollywood depicts truth in its twisted way. Demons do have time on their side. They have nowhere to go but here and they can generally out weight our promises, our covenants, our hopes, dreams and our secrets.

Demons can lay in wait for three generations before coming out to play. As long as they have other demons to hide behind and hold onto when we shake things up spiritually, they have a comfortable home with no rent to pay. The only way to get them out is to have an experienced demon chasing man or woman of God or this exercise to come along to flush them out.

In an earthquake when things start to shake, what do you do? You start to garb for anything that is not moving and that will support or cover you. Demons look to hide behind the secret sin that we won't confess, so by nature of our pride and secrecy, they have job security.

Once we are able to confess and expose that secret sin and expose their hiding place, then they
Seek shelter elsewhere.

EVICTION PROCEEDINGS AT THE DAY SPA

One of the best exercises you can do for your spiritual and mental well-being is what I call a Soul Cleansing Tour. Here's the Purpose, The Process and The Payoff.

THE PURPOSE

The purpose is to free your soul of all the resentment and sinful thoughts that clutter our spirit after days and months of constant rehearsal. By rehearsing these thoughts they become our words; the these spoken words become our actions; these actions become our habits; the habits soon become so comfortable to us that they eventually become or character; then this character has become empowered to carve and determine our destiny.

By going through the day and retraining your thoughts and motives to bless God in thought, in spoken word and in deed, we can retrain our mindset and eventually our destiny. Now that our habits and character has changed, we can successfully flush out the hidden demons who have taken up secret residence on our soul.

121

THE PROCESS

For some who are desperate to make a change in their life, this personal revolution within can be accomplished in one day. Not to sound trite but as we have discussed, a revolution requires desperation and timing in order to occur. If this is your season and you are desperate for a change, you can do this.

Here's how it works. ON the average we think through our life as we travel, walk, work, eat, meditate and sleep. Most of the things that bother us will take up a large portion of that conscious and unconscious time. During this time God is being shut out due to the emotional connection we have to these things rather than the spiritual significance God wants us to interpret them as.

So through these emotions we argue with people who aren't there and we curse them, cry at them and yell at them. After all this is said and done, there is no change because the source has not been confronted and dealt with, you. Yes, I said you. The space between your ears is a vital piece of real estate and as such you should not let just any thought or person in there. *If you learn how to master the effect of people on you, your life would be much more fulfilling and productive.*

Start the day off about 15 to 20 minutes earlier than usual. During this time begin to thank God for all the positive things He has allowed to occur in your life. If you're not sure of what some of those things are, you can immediately tell that this is going to be a multi-day process for you.

Become more familiar with an immediate top ten list that He has spared you from or has blessed you with despite the fact that you are struggling at this moment; get on Google and do a few searches. Your first search if you have children should be; top ten issues affecting children worldwide. The next search if you are single and alone should be top ten issues affecting women in your age group worldwide. Lastly, if your life has been an absolute fairytale with whipped cream and cherries then Google the biggest fears of women in your age group.

You will be amazed about what other women around this globe must contend with on a daily basis. Spend some time researching your peer group across the seven continents and see how good you have it after all. Now let's begin. After you have thanked God for all that He has done for and through you; begin to worship Him for all that he is.

Tell Him how wonderful and gracious He has been to your mind, your body and your soul. Thank Him for sparing your mind when you thought you were going to lose it. Tell Him how grateful you are for sparing the lives of your loved ones and friends. Then just start to speak of His power and ability to be so perfect, powerful and loving to our sinful lives at the same time.

If you have ever done this before then you will know the feeling that will come upon you. You will quite literally be in His presence. You see when you engage in pure worship, this act lifts you from your current state of mind and situation and brings you to the throne of God where you can lay before Him at His feet.

At this moment whatever is plaguing your life must be placed in a state of complete healing or suspended animation. At this very moment in your life, you are completely whole. Here is where you make your commitment to the Lord of hosts about your day. This day you will go through your activities and situations in a state of praise and service. If you have done so before, I can almost promise you that you haven't done it this way. As you pass people on the street, in your car, or whatever mode of

123

transportation you use; you will bless them silently in your spirit as you pass them. I usually alternate between these three phrases.

"Lord, please bless them mightily", Lord, save their soul and heal their body" or I will simply say, *"Lord change their path and give them a spirit to serve you"*. Surely if you are driving you won't catch every car truck or bus that you pass. The interesting thing is you can certainly touch more lives than you are touching now. As I pass school campuses, I pray that the Lord dispatch a guardian Angel to sit upon the tallest building to watch against violence and evil spirits. I bless each child who attends that school and their parents. *I pray for the children who have no one to pray for them as well.*

As I pass churches, I pray that the anointing of God rests heavily upon the Pastor and that all those who enter are transformed and delivered forever. I also pray that the church extend its evangelical reach deep into the community it serves. When I see trucks with names of companies as well as the many business I pass, I pray for their mission and that it is prosperous and that it is eventually molded to suit His Kingdom agenda.

When I encounter people who appear to be struggling in their spirit from my ability to discern, I ask the Lord to lift their spirit above their circumstance so that they can see clearly and Godly for enough time to make sound judgments.

As you can see this is a consciousness that erodes the selfishness that drives our every waking thought. Even if we think of our families and loved ones on a daily basis, we tend to only think of our families and loved ones; not the ones that we never meet but know they exist. They exist with physical pain, and emotional strife on a daily basis.

Our worse day is better than their best day on almost any given day. How often do we take five-minutes and pray for those who have no fresh water to drink this week. How about the victims of human trafficking? How often do we pray for them and their families who fear that they will never see them again?

At some point of the day you will feel the drain from putting out such Godly virtue for those who you don't know. *This is when you start to pray for the ones you do know. Think of it this way, even the boss or the co-worker you dislike is someone's husband, wife, mother, father, son, daughter, brother or sister, just like you. Remember, there were times that you spent even more energy cursing and arguing with the people in your life in your mind.*

You are actually using less energy; just like working out at the gym, you feel more of a burn and the ache because you are using a different muscle group. Each time you work a different muscle group you feel more fatigue quicker because you are not use to using those muscles. In this case you are using a higher level of spiritual consciousness so therefore you will feel uncomfortable and wearier than usual.

Let's not forget the cast of usual suspects. The enemy of man and his cohorts are not pleased that you are looking to make a radical change in your conscious mind toward the mind of God. So they will want to attempt to discourage you from making such a move. Especially when you attempt to bless your co-workers and your adversaries boss and the other people in your life you may deem as hateful. This may feel like an all-out war against you. But here's the fact; satan is a dead man walking who has not been pronounced dead yet.

He has already been defeated; he is just trying to cause as much collateral damage as possible. The ultimate plan here is to flush out the hidden demons in your life that keep in you in bondage. They know that if you clean out your mind of all the negative thinking that cause sickness, diseases and death that they will no longer have anything to hide behind.

They will not be able to hide or hold on to anything once your soul starts to shake and quake every time you feel a touch from God like they use to. Before when you felt the anointing of God in your life, you still didn't change your mind-style so therefore your lifestyle remained the same.

You still kept thinking the same way and doing the same things. Your momentary touch from God was like your visit to the health spa. You may have been transformed temporarily from stressed to at peace, but eventually your nature of doing things got you right back to where you are naturally.

Now that you have gone through a full day of blessing the people God has allowed to cross your path; now you can begin to see the supernatural happen like the parting of the Red Sea. If you have children living with you, then make sure you anoint them and seek God's protection and covering of their soul before you do the next thing. In fact if you can do this without kids in your immediate surrounding then please try to do so.

Next, you will need to be totally transparent before God as you will now commence to call out every secret sin and addiction that you know you have by name. You will then plead the blood of Jesus against this sin and throw a scripture of God's word on that sin to further subdue it.

With that sin uncovered, you will then declare the Lord remove that spirit from your life forever. Here is an example.

"Father God in the name of Jesus I come against the spirit of lust that has been secretly controlling most of the thoughts in my day. Demon of lust I plead the Blood of Jesus against you, by the authority of Jesus Christ I command you to lose your

hold on me right this very second in the name of Jesus. In the name of Jesus, spirit of lust I remand you back to your spiritual source under captivity as commanded by Jesus of Nazareth,. Jesus, you said whatever I bind on earth shall be bound in heaven by the Lord of Hosts. In Jesus name!"

Say this prayer for each of the strongholds in your life; then the moment of truth. Say this; *"Father, in the name of Jesus I know that you are able to do exceedingly and abundantly above all I can think or comprehend, so therefore Lord by your authority given to me, I declare that the demon that is buried deep in my soul that has gone overlooked over all this time be finally exposed and rebuked.*

Father God find that demon that you know by name and cast him down to captivity. Curse his existence to its core and render him harmless as you remove him from my life and shield every life I touch from him manifesting in this life ever again. In Jesus name! Lord I declare that my life is a gift from you, so therefore I render my body and life a gift to you for your eternal service. In Jesus name! Amen that sin

THE PAYOFF

My beloved sister, this is what you call house cleaning to the highest degree. If you make it a point to do this on a consistent basis, you will find a supernatural change has taken place in your life forever. You don't have to do this every day, but you can certainly elevate your mind so that you can get into the habit of blessing people regularly.

This is a mindset that pleases the Lord and brings Him glory. This is how you truly show the Lord you love. Jesus admonished those who would say they loved Him by telling them to show it by keeping His commandments. You can keep His commandments best by loving the Lord with all your heart and loving your neighbor as you love yourself.

This exercise is how you ride your life of the secret sin and the generational curses that ride our spiritual coat tails for years and years undetected. I teach an enhanced four-hour workshop on breaking generational curses and you can find out more about this workshop on my website www.thepowerofperspective.net.

FOR SINGLE PARENTS

This portion of this chapter will be a book unto itself in a future Power of Perspective book title. Being a single parent to me is singularly the most challenging task next to living a saved life. Unless you are free from resentment, anger and fear; single parenting can also raise you up to be a bitter parent and turn your children into feeling every emotion against you that you feel toward your children's father and the circumstances that bring you here.

My reason for saying such harsh words is that it is almost impossible to hide these emotions from the people you love the most. Often times we strike out from the pain of these emotions toward those we love the most.

THINGS TO REMEMBER

Your child did not ask to come here under the circumstances they arrived. Nor did they plan the choices in your life that were made. Anyway you desire to call it, your children are a gift to you from the Lord. Your gift back to Him is how you raise them to serve Him as adults. In my first book, The Power of Perspective Number One, I cover an entire chapter on raising children from a Godly perspective under real and relevant situations in real and applicable ways. Here is some of that wisdom.

Parents are the backbone of the posture we take in life. Without strong parenting, a child is presented to almost every situation from a position of weakness. They are not sure how to process what they are experiencing or how to react. They then become unsure and lose even more confidence if the outcome is a negative one.

Regardless if you are encountering "Baby Momma Drama", or "Baby Daddy Drama", your child deserves better than your excuses. If you have made mistakes in the past that have caused you to get to this position, then you need to repent to God and your ex-spouse and ask them for a chance to be a part of your child's life. Your child didn't make those mistakes for you and they should not be penalized for your errors.

If you are the parent who is in control of the visitation and you know deep down in your soul that your child needs the other parent and the other parent wants to help, then you should also do the godly thing and stop punishing them. What if God were to call you out and expose you for every mistake you make? This is a sobering thought when you realize that in God's eyes we are merely steps ahead, if at all, of those we judge and treat with scorn.

While on this topic, let me share a huge piece of insight the Holy Spirit gave me when my sons were born. He said to pray for their friends, classmates, teachers, instructors, first sweet heart crushes, future girlfriends and wives. I repeat myself for good reason. The enemy repeats his lies, so we should also repeat God's truths. By praying for the lives that will touch your child's, you are purchasing the best insurance policy against the pain and bad experiences you have undergone.

You are asking God to shield that person against the harm that they may inflict on your child as a result. You are asking God to keep and nurture that person the same way He would keep your child. Imagine this, your prayer on that person's behalf may be the only prayer that person ever receives in their lifetime.

When your child experiences that teacher, friend or lover, they will be spared all the baggage and harm that the enemy wants them to face. Your prayers may even cause circumstances to change so that your child may not even encounter that individual. But if they do, you will know that you sent the Holy Spirit ahead to their path to make it smoother.

Don't keep your child under lock and key and prisoner to your fears that they may end up screwed over and abused the way you possibly were. Release them to God's unchanging and eternal hand of guidance and protection. Otherwise, you run the risk of short circuiting their emotional and social development, the two key ingredients to being able to serve God as an adult. He can safeguard your child better than you ever can. Take it from me, I know firsthand. I love my boys more than life itself, but out of a lack of emotional control, my words may have caused damage that my heart couldn't prevent. The Lord has protected their innocent souls and ears and caused healing before I was ever aware of the possibility of pain.

Here is a prayer for safety to say with or for your child. I'm sure you already pray with them, but if you don't, you should start. The enemy has them as a captive audience at school, through TV and music and also walking through the grocery store. Please make this prayer your own by shortening and changing it to suit you and the needs of your child.

"Father God, in the name of Jesus, I thank you for your grace and mercy upon me and my house. I thank you for the care and nurturing your hand has shown me and my family. I thank you for your faithfulness to our prayers and needs. Father, I

thank you for the opportunity to call you God and master over our lives and the privilege of parenthood.

Father, I ask that you wash everything from me and my household that is unlike you. Father, wash me of my sins and sinful tendencies. Make me a clean vessel that may be used for your miracles, signs and wonders. Father, I pray that you dispatch your angelic hosts of protection over my Child (name).

Father, keep him(her) safe from harm always. Keep a hedge of protection around (name). Lord, cause no harm or sickness, injury illness or death to come near them. Keep them covered under your blood. Father, I ask that you keep them safe and order their footsteps and their interaction with others. Guard their heart, mind, body and Spirit and cause your favor, grace and mercy to fall heavily upon them.

Father, protect their innocence from evil spirits with demonic agendas. Consume them with your peace and glory and prevent them from any self-inflicted harm as due to negligence or foolery. Father, protect them from those who may unintentionally cause them physical or emotional harm including myself.
Keep a hedge around them emotionally from any harsh words that may be spoken by me or any loved one due to trying circumstances. Father, keep balance in their lives and a spirit of wisdom and good judgment in their hearts. Continue to fortify me with the wisdom and good counsel that is required of me as a parent.

Please continue to show your faithfulness to us as pledge our hearts and souls to you daily. Please do so and we will be careful to give you the praise and thanksgiving that you and you alone deserve. In Jesus name. Amen.

There are times that you may only have a moment to pray for your child to either encourage their faith or yours either in the middle of the day or in passing. In this case simply say: **"Father, you are truly the God of all creation. I thank you for (name). I pray that you continue to show him/her the care and protection** *tha*t *every situation they encounter may require in Jesus name I pray, Amen".*

These precious lives didn't ask to come here amidst our bad choices and failed relationships. Children are on loan to us from the Lord until they are old enough to serve him on their own as adults. Let's try not to give Him back any damaged goods

RESOLVING CONFLICTS

This is probably a section we all could have used a lesson on before we started dating. The key to maturity and resolving conflicts is not in avoiding them, but understanding how to successfully navigating your way through them. If you are an adult with principles and a methodology to everything you do in life, you are going to have a conflict or two come your way.

As stated before, the real estate between your ears is too valuable to have just anyone or anything occupy unauthorized space there. The key to navigating yourself through most conflicts is one of the following:

1. Your level of maturity?
2. Your level of respect for the other person?
3. Your level of love for the other person?
4. How much of your principles are you willing to sacrifice?
5. What do you expect the outcome to be?
6. What is the value of peace with this person worth to you?
7. How much emotion and pain are you willing to invest?

There are some couples who never argue because they have the discipline to scroll through the above list before they even get into the argument. In fact some individuals assess each relationship in their life according to the above list so they won't get into an argument with them ever. By determining that you will not lose your temper and start to scream regardless of what half of the battle you won. The other half is realizing that emotions don't win anything except your perception of them.

When someone has hurt you and they are close to you, start off the conversation by saying that you need to get something off your chest because you love, like or respect them too much to let this issues that you are encountering to drive a wedge between the two of you. Let them know what happened. Then with love and self-control (without unnecessary emotion) explain what was done. The art of doing this successfully is making it plain to them the difference between:

1. What was done
2. How it made you feel
3. How much they mean to you

Most arguments take place as a result of hurt feelings causing offense and the ensuing back and forth retaliation to outdo each other. When the initial response is anger, it is always best to count to ten and walk away for a moment and then approach the issue with cooler minds. There are a whole lot of people who are on probation, in the hospital, in prison, the cemetery and death row because they didn't count to ten, walk away or give it time to approach the situation with a cooler heads.

The point many of us fail to observe and internalize is that the enemy wants us all dead. Foolish behavior simply grants his request without much work at all. In fact having a bad temper and being intimidating isn't even the ultimate equalizer for a fight. The ultimate equalizer is the person who has nothing to lose. The enemy can conveniently match your temper with someone who has a gun and won't think twice to use it.

From the standpoint of maturity, ask yourself this question; "When I'm 85 years old, how much of what I'm about to say and do is really going to matter? That's why the saying is "Hindsight is 20/20." If we could do it all again we would see things a lot differently, much clearer. If you choose to diffuse, you are also choosing to handle things the way that Christ would.

REMEMBER TO SAY I'M SORRY

Nothing shows humility better than one's ability to say I am sorry. For some no mouthful of words is harder to choke down than those three words. The wonderful thing about saying I'm sorry much like choosing to forgive someone, is the burden that instantly lifts from your spirit. Not forgiving is the baggage you hold in your spirit against someone else.

Avoiding saying I'm sorry is the baggage in your spirit against yourself. Once you say I'm sorry you release your spirit from the bondage of pride that says, "I don't want anyone to have anything on me. It's okay for others to err and show weaknesses, but I don't want them to see mine. I'm not sure that I like the fact that they may see me for what I truly am instead of how I want them to see me." Once again, the important thing here is to remember that your walk on the path of purpose is not at all about you. Your walk is all about being consistently in position to be used by the Lord in a heartbeat.

When you truly sell yourself out for purpose, you don't mind what people think about you after your apology because you have already predetermined your value. You have killed and memorialized the old you that only seeks to self-serve and gain recognition. The new you has been redeemed in the blood of Jesus and is on display as a witness and appreciating in value until His return.

So therefore you are not looking for the validation or assurance from the erratic world around you. Furthermore, your apology speaks up for the true spirit of humility in you. This humility boasts to all the heavenly hosts and the Lord that you truly love Him and desire to serve with Him, in spite of the pain and pride that it costs you.

During this time that you are single there is so much to teach your mind that you will truly forget that you are single.

CHAPTER SEVEN

EXPAND YOUR HORIZONS

You must become what you wish to attract

THE BASICS

*N*othing stimulates a relationship of any kind better than having an engaging and informed conversation. Growing our knowledge base doesn't necessarily involve going back to school or blowing the budget by joining everyone's book of the month club. You can gain knowledge simply by reading. In this age of information, it is pretty hard to be totally ignorant to anything.

You can simply pull up a search engine on your computer and type in any subject matter and there will be an authority on that subject to pop up on your screen. Surely not everything you find on the internet is factual, just be sure to check the source of the information to ensure that the information is from a reputable source. Just because it is on the internet doesn't mean that it's true. I can post a website called the ten sacred truths about North Korean leadership and they could be completely false.

Always make sure the source is a reputable one. If you are looking for information on North Korean Leadership don't trust Yahoo Answers or Ask.com. Trusted sources would be National Geographic and other sources related to the subject. *Anyone can make an internet posting nowadays. With that being said you should still read the internet. It is free, convenient and as long as you check the source, it can be very informative.*

Another great way of gaining information on things and people is by watching and listening to sources such as National Public Radio (NPR), PBS, C-SPAN, National Geographic TV, United Press International and the Associated Press. If your budget permits, there are great books to read that will give you great insight on human character and how we work, change and overcome.

There are a myriad of books to choose from. Some are; *The Tipping Point* by Malcolm Glad well, also *Blink; The Power of Thinking without Thinking*, is also by Malcolm Glad well. Both of these books discuss human psychology and social psychology. Both topics are very entertaining and stimulating to share in conversation.

Try to avoid heavy politics and too much religious dogma. Both topics are extremely slanted and will label you very quickly as a close minded small person. *The Shack* by William P. Young is another book that will stir the imagination and stimulate your peripheral thinking muscles simultaneously. I suggest these books as examples of how to stretch your thinking beyond your belief systems. The reason why the church is so limited is because we judge that which we do not understand.

The word for that is called prejudice. The Sadducees and Pharisees of Jesus' day were the same way. They were respectful law abiding people who chose to remain ignorant and steeped in **FEAR, TRADITION** and **IGNORANCE**; the corner stones of modern day evangelical faith. Reading more material will grow your mind and sharpen your thinking and reasoning skills, because you will have more of a base to reason from.

This new information base will help you dispel myths and ignorance within the body of Christ where ever you fellowship. In fact the mate you are looking for may be in that think tank of minds you will share in. It is said that you need to reach for the level you wish to achieve. The people you associate with are a reflection of you in the way they think and the way they carry themselves. If you find this to not be the case, then you need to examine the company you keep a bit closer.

LOOK AROUND "YOU"

This is where I restate my disclaimer that apologizes in advance for any insult that is taken from the subsequent words. My intent is to never offend you but lift your thinking a little higher and wider. The people you spend personal time with are a good representation of where you are going. The people you wish to meet one day will judge you by the company you keep. Think about it,, the same ignorance you are judged by is the same ignorance you may one day be able to remove by raising your intellectual abilities. I have several female friends who vacation together, shop together and eat together. When they get together they all behave differently than they would if they were alone.

Guys do the same thing, especially when we are in our 20's. There is absolutely nothing wrong with having a good time and even being loud and crazy as long all is done in good taste and within the witness of being a Christian, if you are one.

The ironic thing that I find about hanging out in large groups is that this is when ladies tend to go where there are single men in large numbers. I find that the women who are in these groups tend to be looking for eligible men to date. The concern is, most eligible men try to avoid these type of groups.

Think about it, would you like to date a man who feels comfortable approaching large groups of women in a flirtatious manner? If so then let me caution you that from a man's perspective, the only redeeming quality about approaching a group of women is the fact that you are looking for and will probably get the good time you are looking for. Men of quality are not looking for a serious relationship in those kinds of settings.

Now if you are just looking to exercise your feminine wilds and want to test out your "stuff" then in the company of others is the place to do this safely. Just as always, be mindful of expectations and outcomes. Don't play a game unless you are well familiar with the nature of the players and the rules. Lastly, always know in playing games, there is always a loser; and as children we can always recall that some participants are sore losers.

While out with friends, even if they are all Christians and you are just out having some fellowship time; be mindful of your surroundings. We are in a spiritual war and the enemy never takes a coffee break but he certainly loves Starbucks and other places for casual conversation. If you have never done any of the suggested spiritual exercises in this book, don't be surprised if the man of your life stumbles upon your path.

DRESS THE PART

My sister, I say this and all that I have shared thus far, with love and caring. Regardless of how shy and wholesome a man comes off as being, there is something about you that attracted him. Remember that always!

I'm not chiming in on the phrase that "all men are dogs", because I have met my share of women with the same intent as men but worse, because they planned out every detail before we even said hello. Men just aren't that interested and detailed to begin with. *If your friend is just as cute, our odds just increased by 50%. By knowing that he was attracted to you for something is a good thing. Your question should be, what?*

If it is obvious and you are blessed with stunning looks and/or the body those boys' dreams are made of then please make sure you have some substance between your ears to back that up. As dumb as men can pretend to be, we all admit that if we want this meeting to go beyond the anticipation of sex and/or intermittent booty calls, that there must be something sincere and challenging that needs to come out of her mouth.

As saved as we all want to think we are, the only sinless creation was Christ PERIOD. We all want something from the opposite sex. Maybe it's just good conversation. If so then your cleavage should not be big enough to hide my wallet. Maybe you just want a companion to accompany you from time to time.

Whatever your expectation is for speaking to this man right now, make sure you tell him what that expectation is. Especially as we get into our 40's, we don't have time to waste on miss-information and confusion due to inappropriately setting expectations. If there is a clear attraction, just make it plain what you both want.

Don't get me wrong, all men want something nice to look at. But we don't need to be distracted either. Trust me when I say that we have X-ray vision when we want to use it.

Wearing something tasteful yet flattering is more than enough. We can see the curves even if you wear surgical scrubs and a long sweater. If you are well endowed and you want a man to actually know the color of your eyes and what you are actually talking about then you should not have the twins screaming at us for attention. We actually find it amusing when you keep tugging on your top or jacket to cover your breasts when they never had a chance to begin with when you put that outfit on.

Another distraction is wearing a skirt that barely covers your subject matter. Again, it is amusing when you keep tugging on your skirt to pull it down that additional .02 centimeters. If the skirt or blouse makes you self-conscious enough to keep tugging at them, that is a good indication to leave it at home or give it away. By this time a guy has already made the decision based on your overall presentation if he will introduce you to his friends and family or just keep you, the new "hottie", all to himself. Use discretion in selecting your clothes for the evening or occasion. *Ask yourself what kind of impression of yourself do you wish for him to get.* With all due respect, please, please, please don't wear something that grabs too much in certain areas.

We all can stand to lose a few pounds but if you want to wear a tight bottom to display your assets then be conscious of the fact that the world may be aware of the pattern in your panties or the thickness of your G-string. *Let's face it, truth isn't always flattering.*

Tight pants or tights often show the other components that make up your shapely bottom, like cellulite. Also be very conscious of what pops up when you bend over. I've seen my share of porno movies in the supermarket and had to explain to my two young boys why this woman's entire backside is showing and why she isn't wearing any underwear or a bra. I'm grown enough to know that women who dress like that desire the attention they get and would probably not read a book like this anyway. My hope is that you don't become one of them.

My purpose for writing this book is to hopefully coach you into seeking the right answers to fill-in the blanks in your life and to further clarify that which you already had a clue about. But please understand, my desire is to not judge or insult anyone. We all have needs in this life and we all essentially want the same thing; it's just some of us go about it a different way.

I want to speak to you and treat you the same way I treat all the women in my life and even the ones I meet for the first time, like the way I would want to be treated. Many of us never had the guidance to instruct us about some of the details in life like how to be a lady and how to make certain decisions about the company we keep and the criteria for the people we date.

Some ladies may have been too hard headed to listen to their mothers or fathers and as life rolled along, they found themselves desperately seeking that wisdom from someone. Maybe mom and dad are no longer around or your pride keeps you from asking. In either case just know that you are not alone. Most of the men walking this earth could have used a couple of more years of strong male mentoring. I spend a few hours each month mentoring young boys of all ethnicities and I find they all have the same thing in common. They want to do the right things but don't know how to balance the right thing with being accepted. Just like you at this age, a young man or grown man's worse thought is to be all alone. Although being single doesn't bother men as much as it does women, we still want to feel like we belong; even if it's just with the fellas.

Getting back to my point of packaging, here are some other do's and don'ts to keep in mind relative to appearance.

1. Don't wear blouses that have make-up stains on the collar. If this always happens to you during the day, then you are wearing too much make-up and you need to be more careful in how you wear your garments.

143

2. Don't wear t-shirts or blouses that show all the rolls on your side. If it looks too tight when you put it on, it will be just as tight during the day.

3. If you are not comfortable in high heels and you were never taught how to walk in them properly, then try wearing heels an inch or so shorter. Nothing creates a spectacle more than a woman who looks awkward walking in heels.

4. Check your hose regularly for runs and always have a backup or some clear coat polish to catch a run. Some men, like yours truly can catch a glimpse of everything about you including the run at the heel of your sling backs within the same amount of time it takes you to look at your watch.

5. If you must wear acrylic nails please maintain them by getting a fill or a color change in the timely manner they require. If you want a man that takes care of himself, you better believe that he wants the same of his woman. I understand that you may get busy at times, but this is the time to consider removing the nails until a time you have more time to care for them.

6. On the topic of nails, please show the same care to your feet and legs. If you need a pedicure then don't wear open toe shoes or sandals. No one is going to ask you why your feet are in that condition, they will simply assume that you don't care that much about your appearance. All it takes is two more minutes to put on some lotion or apply some nail polish remover to take off the chipped color. Going bare is better than going chipped.

7. ***The best thing you can wear that goes with everything is a genuine smile.*** Nothing strikes a chord better than a smile. Many of us don't put one on as much as we should because it may be miss-understood or we forget. Who cares what they think. Smile because you look good doing it.

I'm sure most of these may strike you as common place or even odd, but to someone who has never been told this before, it was on time. You can't assume that everyone knows what you know. There are certain aspects to American culture that our neighbors throughout the world don't follow or understand. In the same regard there are things that we may not know about etiquette that are quite common place in other parts of the world. If we isolate our thinking we become like the Pharisees and Sadducee's that helped to crucify Jesus.

BECOME WELL ROUNDED

You don't necessarily have to own seasonal ticket for the Metropolitan Opera or The Philharmonic, but you should at least know where they are located and what they are for. It's part of being well rounded. The same thing goes for knowing the difference the placement of such terms as 1st down, pick 'n roll, bunt, check and the Heisman. It doesn't only apply to sports. You should also know where these names reside;

1. Mahmoud Ahmadinejad
2. Dmitry Medvedev
3. Kim Jong Il
4. David Cameron
5. Carlos Slim

Being well rounded doesn't make you the expert it just makes you reasonably informed. Don't use the phrase, "I'm not into that stuff" as your excuse for not being willing to learn. By not expanding your horizons you are saying that I am pleased in the level of ignorance that I have. If you also are stuck in your ways and don't want to change along with not wanting to learn new things, then you will find yourself alone a great deal of the time.

As we get older, we have a tendency to put up with less and don't want to jump through any more hoops or change just to please somebody. You don't have to wear purple and yellow highlights in your hair but being willing to meet someone half way is just plainly the nice thing to do. In order to have friends you must first show yourself to be friendly.

If you want to be loved, you must first also be loveable. Being a nice person also makes for good witnessing if you are Christian. If you can't successfully win someone to you, then how can you win them to Christ? We have all sorts of reasons as to why we won't adapt to or accept new things, yet we want things to get better for us and the folks we love. Most of us just have an aversion to change itself.

Here's another excerpt from my devotional Snack Food for the Soul. This one is called:

BE THE CHANGE...

The Full quote is *"You must be the change you wish to see in this world"*. These life changing words are associated with Mohandas Gandhi, a political and ideological leader in South Africa and India in the 1930's and '40's. Gandhi is best known for being a thought leader who was ahead of his time. Gandhi believed in the equal rights for all ethnicities and their gender despite their political orientation. As an attorney and political reformer Gandhi believed in holding political leaders accountable to their elected positions to serve. As a devout Buddhist and Hindu he was committed to pursuing purpose and discovering truth.

At the start of a New Year we are all at some point or another forced into a reflective mode as we look at our lives over the past year and what we wish to change and pursue in the New Year. The New Year is the time we remember those who have passed from this life to the next as well as those we had to part company with for any number of reasons. We also are in need of knowing that we are on the right track and that if we were to leave this life that we will leave a legacy or some positive trace that we were here.

Our inherent trait as Believers is to ask our Savior to make changes and accommodations in our world on our behalf, but seldom are we as eager to change ourselves in order to accommodate the world.

Jesus had to experience this discomfort of conforming to accommodate many times in His ministry. Even though He spent 30 years preparing for 3 ½ years of ministry Jesus Himself still had to fast and pray to embody God's wisdom and anointing. Jesus regularly performed miracles to raise man's spiritual consciousness while knowing His ultimate sacrifice was near.

Jesus became love to overcome hate and became hope to over shadow despair. When the law called for death, He became the example of grace so that sinners' lives would be spared. When order was needed He became the rebuke that silenced the rampaging tongues. When tenderness was needed there was always oil nearby to soothe.

When the time came to pay up for the penalty of our sins, He became the sacrifice that paid it all in full. During these new and innocent days of the New Year as we move more delicately and methodically let us also consider some Soul Improvement in our laundry list of resolutions this year.

Let us consider becoming the miracle that is needed by counteracting the void. If it is love we are in need of, let us first become loving to each other, even when it's not convenient to our pride and ego. If it's healing we need, let us remember that He took on the scars for our healing and was chastised for the sake of our peace. Let's seek the quiet place and time to embody God's wisdom and anointing so that we can lay hands on ourselves and profess our own healing.

When the enemy's manifestations seem to prevail, let us become the living epistles that are soaked in the darkness chasing demon slaying word of God. If there is no class, integrity or Godliness in your place of employment, then become the elegant, transparent child of God that the Lord saved you to be. The wisdom of the laws of attraction pre-date Christ in this world. If you become what you want the world immediately around you to become, then it has already changed because of your intent.

The blessing you desperately desire has been custom tailored by the love of God just for you; so therefore that same blessing is in the spiritual realm seeking you as well. By becoming the change you wish to see in this world will put you in position to receive that blessing.

God's laws of reciprocity work a little differently than ours. In fact they operate in the complete opposite of our reasoning. ***In order to receive you must first release.*** To be in position to receive God's anointing and favor has nothing to do with a physical position at all but everything to do with your a spiritual 24/7.

In 2011 let us counteract this downward spiral that our society has taken. Instead of talking about what should take place, *let us take that place and become what should be, by changing one mind at a time by our incessant and consistent pursuit.*

I couldn't resist sharing another Snack Food devotional that seems to fit the theme of adapting and growing for the better.

WHO'S HOLDING YOU BACK?

If I had a dollar for each time I posed a threat to someone because of how I carried myself, I would retire wealthy right now. That statement can be construed of confidently factual or arrogant. In either case there is a glimmer of truth. In almost every job that I've held since the age of 16, I've encountered someone who is referred to colloquially as a "Hater".

Haters are people who despise you for the greatness you NATURALLY possess or the image or status you have achieved. I used caps for the word naturally because like etiquette training some people can be molded to impersonate greatness but only the God given trait of greatness becomes your nature.

When the individual who is impersonating greatness becomes desperate they will logically resort to their nature; and if their nature is not of the caliber of Godly greatness then they will subvert their own elevation. Take for instance the names of some of the celebrities our western culture exalt to the status of greatness.

From the very start as we raise them higher we begin to see the cracks in their character. As soon as they are faced with the same adversity you and I have to contend with on almost a regular basis, they completely fracture and create a mess around them. The fact is they didn't belong up there to begin with.

People who have the innate spark of greatness that was spoken into existence by God seem to instinctively know it. Even when everyone seems to get their blessing you remain at peace because there is a validation that is yours that didn't come from man. It's almost as if the Holy Spirit told you a secret that only the two of you share.

So, "Who's holding you back?" Is there still some obstacle that systematically blocks your success or your ability to get to that level you know God called you to? Is it that you secretly feel that you're not good enough, or that you don't fit the profile of true success?

Giving credit to whom credit is due, I recently had the pleasure of meeting Bishop George Bloomer. Besides being a gifted preacher and teacher, Bishop Bloomer is a highly acclaimed author and is world renowned for being transparent and candid; two essential character traits for winning souls to Christ.

Bishop Bloomer taught on God's selection process for His chosen King of Israel, David. This topic would not be properly justified without including Bishop Bloomer's perspective. Bishop Bloomer's testimonies told of being raised in a rough section of Brooklyn, New York and eventually succumb to the hustle of the streets. The soon to be preacher became a drug dealer and perhaps a party to many other crimes.

Bishop Bloomer never completed high school but he did heed the call upon his life and totally submitted to the call of ministry. To date he has been asked by the Kellogg's company and other fortune 500 companies to teach their leaders. Today Bishop Bloomer is a best-selling author and shepherd's a multi-million dollar ministry that is taking back real estate from our enemy.

I referenced Bishop Bloomer's story to illustrate the point that at face value Bishop Bloomer's background doesn't match his corporate success and acceptance, but when God chooses a vessel, His only qualification for them is that they are available. God chose King David who happened to be the least likely candidate for the position. He was not the stature, nor the aesthetics of a King. But David did stand head and shoulders above his brothers in one characteristic and that was the only one God cared for and that was a shepherd's heart.

By being covered with the stench of dirt, sweat and dung; *David's outward appearance offended man but impressed God;* 1 Samuel 16:7, "But the Lord said to Samuel, Look not on his appearance or at the height of his stature, for I have rejected him. For the Lord sees not as man sees; for man looks on the outward appearance, but the Lord looks on the heart."

Many of the people who now hold the status and prestige you feel you will never achieve may appear clean on the outside but their hearts are offensive to the Spirit of God. God said in His word that "The wealth of the sinner is laid up for the just"

The Spirit of God is about to orchestrate the greatest transfer of wealth and power ever known to man. God is resetting all the rules and the game pieces on the board because of those who have failed and disobeyed Him. The things that you feel disqualify you are no concern to God.

He is looking for available vessels to pour His anointing into and He'll handle the rest; whom He called He also predestined. Even though the people around you don't have the wisdom to see the riches within you don't stop being and doing what the Holy Spirit tells you to be. Do you fit man's profile for success?

The next time you send out invitations to your pity party, here's another perspective; ask the Lord to show you the heart He sees in you. *"If God be for us WHO can be against us?" So, Who's Holding You Back?*

CHAPTER EIGHT

MARRIAGE READY

There are times that you say I do, long before he even says hello.
This tells the Lord that you really are ready, this time.

REALITY

I suppose it would be really disingenuous for me to
write a book about how to be successfully single without
creating a chapter on what the profile of someone who is
marriage ready looks like. If you were to research the top ten
fears of women around the world, one of those that rank near the
top would be the fear of being alone. In fact there are some
cultures where the primary value of a girl to her family is her
financial worth to the family of the boy she will one day marry.

In this culture if a man has several daughters and one or two sons
to help him work he is considered a man of great wealth
potential because his daughters will bring him a hefty sum of
money. Cultures such as these prepare a girl child for marriage
as soon as she is able to do chores.

Her entire makeup is conditioned to watch her mother for the
cues of womanhood. Her adaptation to her calling as a wife will
determine her future happiness. There are other cultures where a
girl child means that the father and mother will be taken care of
well into their senior years because their culture does not believe
in senior or assisted living programs. Taking care of the elders is
considered an honor that primarily falls upon the girl child in the

family. On the flip side of this, history records families praying for the birth of a boy because a boy child will represent that family's potential to earn money.

There are times that horrible stories would surface of families discarding female babies with the trash or taking the infant out to the wilderness and leave her to meet certain death by wild animals. A girl child means another mouth to feed without the hope of income because women cannot work.

As you see there are a great many perspectives in this world on the same subject, you. Right now as we speak there are cultures who believe that the moment a boy can walk and begin to comprehend his father's commands that he should be trained to adapt the skills of what it takes to be a man.

These skills are vital to his survival and ability to protect and care for what will one day be his home. The center of that home is considered his wife. So in essence that boy is being prepared to take care of you. Surprisingly that scenario I just described is not just in some sub-Saharan country in Africa or the Middle East. Some of those cultures are in Israel, Mexico, South America and even in Europe.

On the continent of Africa in most countries the woman is the administrator of the home and is highly revered. The man simply provides but the woman makes it all happen. Sound familiar? This high level of respect for the woman is also prevalent in the Caribbean and South America. Although the woman is not publicly declared the head, behind closed doors it's quite clear who rules the roost. But it's done in a way where everyone under the same roof knows the role they play.

In Asian and middle Eastern cultures the woman is expected to stay home and raise the children and tend to her home. Although she is the center of the family, she is not treated with the same level of respect publicly as her counterpart further to the west. She is not permitted to speak to or acknowledge other men in public and has strict cultural guidelines that she must adhere to when in public such as her dress and protocol.

So why this brief lesson on sociology? This is to illustrate that different perspectives can be introduced into your life at any given time on a subject that you may feel that you are the expert on. Just because you are accustomed to a certain lifestyle or a certain modality of thinking doesn't mean that it is necessarily the only, or the only right way. It just means that you haven't tried anything else.

Stay with me, I'm trying to take you some place new. We in western civilization are the youngest culture on the face of the earth. In comparison to our neighbors in the East such as Africa and Asia that are thousands of years old, American culture is a mere teenager. With that being said, you know the nature of teenagers. Teens are primarily selfish, stubborn, self-righteous, sloppy, belligerent, rude, emotional and driven by pop culture.

These descriptors basically captured the nature of our nation. From the political structure that governs our public and private rights to our so-called moral leaders and corporate executives to our celebrities and athletes that occupy the role of our monarchy.

 We are a country that is more driven by our senses than our sensibility. If you spend one week watching the latest craze we call Reality TV you'll see exactly what I mean. As a single woman who wants the best chance at a happy and fulfilling life you need to consider culture, intelligence and character in your criteria for selecting the man who earns your affections. The bible says when a man findeth a wife he findeth a good thing but the wife needs to be educated on the full selection to choose from. Keep following me, I'm getting there.

PERCEPTION

Have you heard the funny story about a spirit filled man whose town was flooded out by rains? He climbed up to his roof for safety as the water started to rise past his windows. He knew that the Lord would save him. Along came a man in a row boat and told him to jump into the boat for safety. The man refused because the boat was too small. An hour later a man in a bigger boat came by and offered to take him to safety. He refused because the boat was too crowded. Then came a man hanging from a helicopter and he refused him too because it looked too dangerous. Eventually the rains came back harder than before and he eventually drowned. When he got to heaven the man asked the Lord "why didn't you save me?" The Lord replied by saying, "I sent you two boats and a helicopter and you refused all three of them. What were you expecting?"

Sometimes we seek knowledge or help with too many pre-conceived notions. We have become so conditioned and prejudiced in our thinking that when the help comes we miss it entirely because we are too self-absorbed. If you remember, the Jews missed their messiah because they didn't like the way He was packaged.

There are also times that we need to make a major decision but choose not to ask for the advice of someone who has made this choice before. Like teenagers, we convince ourselves that we know what is best for us, instead of finding out what are all the available options. Let's face it we are not teenagers any longer. We need to expand our viewpoint to include opportunities that are not the norm.

Jesus did everything in an unorthodox way. From His arrival into this world His existence and actions stretched man's way of thinking. He chose to teach by illustration and storytelling rather than the wordiness of old doctrinal beliefs. One of my favorite quotes was said by Oliver Wendell Holmes. He said "man's mind once stretched by a new idea never regains its original dimensions." So my dear sister, my objective is to encourage you to also think outside the box relative to the packaging that your ideal man may come in. If you are a single white female looking for your ideal man as six foot three with wavy blonde hair and Caribbean blue eyes and built like an Olympian; you may miss out on the fact that God packaged His ideal man for you as five-foot eleven, Hispanic and a little chubby around the edges. Yes, the bible says the Lord will give you the desires of your heart.

But in this day of unprecedented disobedience, what if the only man who was obedient to the voice of God with the destiny that God wants you to be a part of has these specific looks? Let's face it, God doesn't just stand there like a waiter taking orders to our custom requested deserts. He uses people who are willing and able to be used.

So if the best vessel that suits the desires of your heart and destiny is not a six- foot six NBA player or actor or CEO and it happens to be a five- foot eleven accountant with thinning hair then that is who He will send you. Now if you meet this accountant with the great salary, great credit and devoted heart to God and you refuse him based on his packaging; you can't blame God for missing your blessing like the man in the boat or the Jews.

Needless to say this example of perception may not be acceptable to all but it is to some. Dating outside of one's race takes careful deliberation especially if you know that your family and friends will not be on board with your decision. Sometimes we never know how strongly our very own loved ones feel about race until the likelihood exists of someone from another race actually joining the family or your social circle. Folks such as me who are from the Caribbean are accustomed to having multiethnic representations in our family. So marrying someone Caucasian, Asian, Jewish or Hispanic doesn't bother us in the least. Certainly there are some who feel differently but they are not the majority. My wife happens to be a Caucasian of Polish decent. Although she never had a problem with being around and dating African-Americans, she knew her father did.

She didn't know how much it bothered him and her step-mom until four years into our marriage. They are both very sweet and loving people and embraced my two sons the same way my family embraced her daughter. But there is something to be said about perceptions. There was always an underlying current of resentment and indifference toward us that eventually caused their estrangement from my wife and my daughter.

At the writing of this book the comfort zone of these two children of God is so strong that it is worth missing out on the growth and development of their granddaughter. My wife and I are prayerful that the Lord will open their eyes and heart to the fact that heaven doesn't have culturally indigenous neighborhoods and God isn't concerned with any citizenship other than the body of Christ.

This is just one example of the many stories I'm sure that you have heard or have experienced directly. Dating and marrying outside of your race has nothing to do with what feels right but everything to do with feeling you deserve who will treat you the best and love your God the most. Let's meet Jesus one day knowing that we have overcome the spirit of the Sadducees and the Pharisees.

MARRY CHARACTER BEFORE SPIRITUALITY

Not something that you expected to hear from a minster and teacher, right? Let me explain before your eyebrows shoot through your hairline. Over the last 20 years of ministry I have found that most of the problems within the body of Christ relative to ministry, business and matters of the heart didn't have as much to do with one's salvation as it did for their character and upbringing.

I have seen the most saved and sanctified Christians behave like street corner thugs when engaged in a heated dispute. On the other hand I have seen the unsaved and unredeemed of the Lord conduct themselves as restrained and respectable as you would expect the most seasoned Christian to behave. Why is that?

It has to do with the makeup of the person individually. Someone who was raised in a loving and well balanced environment where values and self-respect are revered more than anything else will often grow up to be that way. Having the Holy Spirit within will only help them to be better.

When times are tough and they are struggling with their salvation they will still have good character to fall back on. But someone who has never been taught "good values" and self-respect may clean up their act when they become Spirit-filled. But when they too struggle with their salvation they won't have as much of a firm foundation to fall back on. I have seen this time and time again

I've encountered cases where the unsaved spouse who was raised to be a good husband held the marriage together while the saved woman was the one to be unfaithful and vice versa. I have also seen that the saved business owner was the one who handled things inappropriately or dishonestly. As always this is not always the case. Jesus is able to change anyone who wants to be changed.

I once mentored a young lady we'll call "Nita." She grew up as a child of incest at the hand of her brother and uncle. As we got to know each other she shared more and more about her past. She had tried various spiritual foundations to base her life on and seemingly had a provocative lifestyle as she described her broad range of experiences sexually and socially.

 She tried drugs and like myself had two failed marriages. She had been shot and experienced first-hand the miraculous healing power of God. She attended a class I was teaching on discipleship and asked me to mentor her because she felt the hand of God on her life to make some serious changes in her lifestyle. Nita told me she has tried everything else and that the Lord has placed a burden for ministry in her heart heavily.

Nita knew that if she didn't change that her kids and grandkids would suffer the spiritual consequences for her disobedience and sinful tendencies by way of a generational curse. Not only that, she also knew what her eternal fate would be for not following the heart of God. Nita now fears failing God more than failing herself. One would say that Nita may not be a primary candidate for a man looking for a virtuous woman from a good family and a righteous upbringing. The fact is that Nita has the best foundation for God to build a new house on; a foundation that is agenda free and desperate for His will in her life.

This kind of person will worry about bringing shame to her God long before she thinks of how to please man. If you find a man with the same kind of heart then with the help of the Lord you both will be fine. Just don't place your future on someone who mimics God.

Remember that satan goes to our churches too and he can also speak in tongues with the best of them. He can disguise himself as an angel of light to deceive you; he wants you distracted and discouraged. It is not too hard for him to send you a mate with a hidden demon so that he can eventually awaken a circumstance that will eventually claim your soul. Woman of God please,

please make sure you pray and seek God before you accept the man that will be your covering.

BLENDED FAMILIES

Nowadays blended families make up almost half of the family structure in our nation. Not planning for such a union can prove to be exhaustive and painful. As a child of a blended family it was painful and exhaustive for me because I didn't want to tell my mother that she married a man with dual personalities for fear that it would create strife in our home, so I kept my issues with him to myself. I strongly recommend that if you are a single parent who eventually marries a man with or without kids that you establish an open communication policy with your children and encourage him to do the same with his.

Then you both need to establish the same pact with your step-children. Many second marriages that are in blended families pull apart because of issues dealing with a difference of philosophies in child rearing as well as issues that are territorially driven.

 At the end of the day as the adults you both need to commit to making it work because that and prayer and devotion time is all that will make it work. I write a Blog for Psychology Today and I was inspired to do a story on blended families because I thought that my personal story would be a blessing to that audience.

It turns out that article received the highest hits of all the articles I've written for Psychology Today. I asked myself for permission to reprint my article in its entirety in my book and I told myself that it would be okay to do so. What can I say; sometimes you have to entertain yourself because you will be the only person who "gets you."

161

The Power of Perspective
Harnessing the power that lies behind seeing life from
different vantage points.
by Sean Cort

HELPFUL ADVICE FOR BLENDED FAMILIES

Blended families require friendship, love and tremendous
understanding.
Published on January 6, 2010

 We all have heard the stats pertaining to the divorce rate of
marriages in the American home. Although the precise
number varies depending on your source, you will find that
the numbers hover around 42 to 49% for the first marriage
then escalates to around 60 to 67% for the second marriage
then jumps again to approximately 74% for marriage
number three. We'll stop there in the interest of brevity, but
there is obviously a trending north of 75% for nuptials 4 and
higher.

 Hopefully those of us who have divorced more than once
have at some point taken an inward journey to asses where
the challenges in our decisions stem. This is certainly not an
indictment or a judgment call from me to anyone. I merely
speak for myself. I've divorced twice and upon deciding to
try for success a third time, there were some non-negotiables
I knew I would have to require as well as some profound
concessions I would need to make. Upon my second divorce,
my wife and I decided that our two sons would be best off
with me. In hindsight I now realize fathering my sons
fulltime was not even a variable up for discussion. I wasn't
going to be the absentee father that my dad was to me.

When you remarry into a family with children or you take
your children into a new family, the choices you make and

the perspective you live will have even more of a compound affect. As a Caribbean born American raised in Brooklyn, New York I chose to marry a Polish American woman raised in a suburb of Chicago, Illinois called Downers Grove.

Her daughter and my sons became fast friends; at the time they were ages 4, 6 and 8. We've since gone through the full gamut as you can imagine living in the South East United States. We've encountered racism in our church, neighborhood and even in our places of employment. Our children have encountered the subtle emotional and psychological abrasions one would expect them to receive from kids who see them attending activities with a parent and siblings of a different race.

We've even encountered friction within our home as a result of our cultural differences and the occasional territorial skirmishes that siblings endure. My wife and I decided to educate our children on all the possible situations they could be faced with so that no one or nothing would catch them unaware. We chose to live in Central Florida. Our scenario alone makes for an interesting reality based television show. My wife and I shared the notion that all human beings want to feel loved and that they belong to someone or something. This family became that unit of love and belonging despite the current of external influences.

We made a vow that we would never treat the other in a manner that we would not want to be treated. Sound familiar? We've made that Golden Rule more relevant on a micro level by adapting the following.

- ✓ It is a non-negotiable that we eat dinner together as a family with the television turned off.
- ✓ We've learned to accept each other as individuals without trying to change them, the same way we will have to accept people in the world outside our home.
- ✓ If change is necessary, we discuss the issue with a clear and concise explanation of its benefits as well as

the penalty for non-compliance both in our home and in life.
- ✓ We take the time to learn each other and appreciate the strengths and challenges we all inherently have and discuss them in a loving and non-judgmental atmosphere.
- ✓ We make appropriate family decisions together so therefore all parties have a stake in the process and outcome.
- ✓ My wife and I vow to keep our major disagreements away from our children with the understanding that we explain that mom and dad do disagree without having to be disagreeable or create a contentious atmosphere
- ✓ We tend to keep short accounts with each other and not let issues build up in layers thus causing a volcanic explosion. We teach our children and each other the type of things that one should easily forgive and let go versus the issues that should be dealt with directly and promptly.
- ✓ We bind together and multiply each other's joys and accomplishments so that we can also divide each other's failings and sorrows.
- ✓ We start and maintain family traditions such as saying I love you at least three times a day and making birthdays and other occasions special. We even make up our own holidays that we keep sacred in our home.
- ✓ Because we are of the Christian faith, we say grace over every meal, even publicly we bow our head in prayer. My wife and I firmly believe that if we teach our children that it is okay to display their belief system publicly then they will seldom be ashamed of who they are.

Certainly there is no magic stair step method to successfully raising a blended family. I'm sure we can all believe in one thing; and that is as people we all want to feel that when we leave this life that someone will benefit from a legacy we've created filled with fond thoughts and memories. If you decide to become a blended family, the memories you'll create are a great place to start.

If this blessed you please feel free to log onto www.psychologytoday.com and type in my name, Sean Cort in the search window on the page. All my most recent articles will come up. You can also access this through my website www.trueperspectivepublishing.com

WATCH YOUR MOUTH

He said, She said: I'll start off with three words of advice in this area, don't do it. Always try to take the high road in this area and in all aspects of your life. Starting with church; this is the breeding place for rumor, gossip and lies. **If you hear it, kill it and move on.** When someone comes at you with the latest edition of *Gossip for Dummies* simply say I don't have the time and you shouldn't either.

 The fact of the matter is, you will be the topic next. Because the rumor mill is an abyss that can never be satisfied. It is baseless and has no form or reasoning other than to consume all it touches. No one gets out of it unscaved, no one.

Men already have the impression that women like to run their mouths about any and everything. Men also feel that women hold grudges and resentment for long periods. To be honest I have found myself to feel the same way about many women I've encountered. My sister and friend, if you have never been told before, please let me tell you now.

Nothing turns a man off more than listening to a woman or anyone for that matter totally unload about someone for something they did years ago with the amount of detail that only a true crazy person would remember. A woman scorned is not a pretty picture.

I've since found out that women are wired with a need to talk things out in great detail even if it occurred years ago or if that thing has nothing to do with them. For instance if Sally bumped into Alice at the mall and sees that Alice is returning half of the outfits that she saw her wear over the last month, she will feel the need to either confront her about the obvious scam that she's pulling or Sally will have to confide in at least four of her closest friends.

Of course these four close friends have four even closer friends that they must confide in as well. There is an old shampoo commercial that aired in the 80's whose slogan was "and so on, and so on, and so on" This proved to the world that women must talk about what they witness or feel.

Men can keep things inside and express that energy elsewhere. Freud termed this masculine ability as employing cathexis and anti-cathexis; this simply means that men can bottle up energy in one area of our lives and expel it in another area. This is mostly done through sexual aggression or through another physical expression such as working out at the gym or kicking the neighbor's dog. I made up the part about the dog. No letters please.

Unfortunately for the fact that women are hard wired as nurturers you can't let anything go that easily. You are made to hold onto things to see them through. So unless you have closure immediately, you will keep rehearsing it in your mind, your spirit and until it affects your body. So physiologically speaking, as a women you will actually get sick if you don't talk things out to completion. Aren't you really hating Eve right now? If you're a feminist, aren't you really hating Adam right now? With all kidding aside, the Lord knows that you need to vent. He is simply saying cast your cares on Him for He truly cares for you. By saying **"greater is He that is in you than he that is in the world"** Jesus is really saying that His love for you is greater than anyone's hate for you. Just as He did in the Garden of Eden, God made provisions before you knew the need. Opening your mouth and spilling your heart on the ground will only implicate you later and leave the man that died for you broken hearted because you keep turning your back on Him.

TOP 10 REASONS TO TRUST NO ONE BUT THE LORD

10. Jesus doesn't text

9. Jesus won't compete with you

8. Jesus knows what it feels like to be betrayed

7. Jesus has no one to impress

6. Jesus isn't into the things you're into

5. Jesus won't get drunk and spill the beans

4. Jesus doesn't mind always paying the check when you eat out

3. His credit is flawless

2. He doesn't need to borrow anything

And the number one reason that you should trust no one but the Lord is…

1. **No one else in your life can keep the things a secret that He knows about you. He loves you enough to allow you the dignity to hold your head up despite the fact that you let Him down. What other man will allow you to do that without holding it against you?**

Now that we are bringing our time together to a close, I want to ask you the same thing I ask the students in my weekly Life Enhancement class that I teach in the church I attend. Did you learn something that you didn't know before you picked up this book? I hope so. If all of this was nothing but a brief review, then I challenge you to share your wisdom. There is a woman somewhere who needs to hear your wisdom in your words.

Here is the fun part. What book to single women from a man would be complete without a list of the things that men love about women? Here we go.

- A woman who is not afraid to smile and say hello
- A woman who is confident in her skin but still personable
- A woman who knows how and when to switch on her masculine side
- A woman who can easily forgive after receiving a sincere apology
- A woman who can make a man feel like a little boy when he wants to
- A woman who can make a man feel like a little boy when he needs to
- A woman who can love a man as unconditionally as his mother use to
- A woman who knows when to be behave sexy, nasty and like the church mother
- A woman who can pray, cry and hold his children when they need to be held
- A woman who can remind him of the things he can never remember
- A woman who doesn't want to be the man
- A woman who can laugh
- A woman who can make him laugh

- A woman who can make him cry
- A woman who can love him passionately enough to frighten him just a bit
- A woman who can make him melt just by looking at him that certain way
- A woman who can speak volumes with her eyes
- A woman who always smells good
- A woman who gets dressed up for no other reason than just because
- A woman who is willing to do anything he wants even though she won't have to
- A woman who doesn't play tit for tat
- A woman who knows him like the back of her hand but doesn't rub it in
- A woman who can keep the house in order even if her life is in disarray
- A woman who can remind him of how it felt when they first met
- A woman who loves Jesus even more than he and knows how to show it
- A woman that knows how to make more out of less with everything
- A woman who can calm him down and think things out carefully
- A woman who is real and not too afraid of being transparent
- A woman who does not gossip or hold grudges against people overall
- A woman who is not emotional or needy
- A woman who can cook and clean but doesn't mind if we don't
- A woman who can stand her ground but remain a lady
- A woman who isn't jealous or insecure

169

- A woman who fits in with anyone without judging them
- A woman who is a great critical thinker
- A woman who makes him feel like her hero

Now, no man is expecting all of these things all the time but it can be helpful to have a thumbnail sketch as to what is actually going on in our minds when we say "nothing."

Finally, my sister and friend I pray that these last few pages have brought a smile to that Jesus kissed face of yours, because you deserve it. I wish that there could be a day that all men in our society as a whole could celebrate and honor you.

Believe it or not, there are millions of men who feel the same way I do. You are more than just mother's day because some may never be a mother nor do they really want to. When I say celebrate you I mean as how God made you in the Garden of Eden. Maybe we'll call it Eve's Day, which will celebrate the way God showed off when He made you. *I'm sorry that life may have thrown you some curves and foul balls. But as hurtful as they must have been, look at you, you're still here.*

I know that you have had some restless moments trying to fathom your next move especially after the fact that things didn't go your way. Have no fear. The God who hung billions of galaxies against the back drop of questions only He can answer, also knows the number of the hairs on your head. Understand that this is the same God that can navigate the space between your ears and the space he desires to fulfill in your heart. He desires more for you than you can possibly think and comprehend.

This is not the close of another uncertain chapter. It isn't even the beginning of another. This time in your life, just is; the same way that He, just is. That's what He wants you to understand.

God, just is; and because of that you will never be less than the reason He said Let there be…

Log onto www.trueperspectivepublishing.com to keep up with other book titles by Sean Cort in The Power of Perspective book series. Future titles will include children's books targeted at self and spiritual-awareness and character development. Future titles will also deal with more specific subject matter dealt with in The Power of Perspective part one.

You may also subscribe to receive by email Snack Food for the Soul, our brief life-enhancing devotional that has literally changed thousands of lives through-out the world. If you are an aspiring author, the True Perspective Publishing House may be the instrument to help you tell your story by eliminating the intimidation from the publishing process. Find out more about how you can leave your literary mark in this life.

If you would like to schedule Sean Cort to speak at your next women's event log on to www.trueperspectivepublishing.comor email our offices at info@trueperspectivepublishing.com

SEAN CORT

Sean Cort is an award-winning veteran with over 25 years of New York market radio, television, advertising and marketing experience. His passion is to sow vision and purpose into each life he touches and as a result has positively impacted every medium for communication today.

 Sean's multi-industry repertoire include titles as promoter, producer, writer and director for venues such as Madison Square Garden, Radio City Music Hall, Carnegie Hall, The Brooklyn Academy of Music, Avery Fisher Hall, The Meadowlands Arena and Central Park. Sean's theatrical resume encompasses voice over work and acting for Broadway, radio, television and film.

In the area of on air talent, Sean has reported, written, produced and hosted programming for AM, FM talk and music shows in Chicago, New York City and Orlando for entities such as PBS, NBC, TBN, Gospel Today's magazine and Crosswalk.com.

Sean's philosophy toward leadership, brand management and church membership is, "If you make people feel special by paying attention to their details and you master the art of expectations management, you will overcome a multitude of imperfections".

Through the Power of Perspective Workshop Series Sean teaches a wide array of topics ranging from How to Adapt and Lead a Diverse Cultural Mix, How Churches Can Refine Their Brand Marketing of Jesus, How to Break Generational Curses by Changing the Way You Think, How to Build Intimacy with God and How to Handle Change.

Sean is a Masters trained and ordained Elder and motivational speaker who has addressed audiences as large as 75,000 people. Sean's devotion to the church body drives him to enlighten the ecumenical community on performing with a spirit of excellence and faithfulness consistently.

His genuine transparency and quick witted humor captivates his audience as his Broadway like stage presence drives his message home every time. Sean is President and Founder of The Healing Continuum.com, a health based initiative designed to increase health literacy for women and the lives they touch. Through this company Sean actively consults physician groups and pharmaceutical companies in areas of patient education, strategic planning and media production.

Sean Cort is also a former consultant with the Disney Institute. In this capacity Sean taught the Disney methodology to success to an exclusive Fortune 100 clientele. His years in senior management with this entertainment icon showed him the need for these services to be offered to the church body as well. Sean now teaches churches, businesses and variousnon-profit organizations the forgotten art of exemplary customer service through expectations management.

Sean is the author of, 'The Power of Perspective' (TPOP). TPOP promises to help you become as intimate with God as you are with your own thoughts. Our thoughts are the nucleus from where our words, actions and character generate. These characteristics determine your destiny.

The included workbook will help you reconcile your past, chart your future and relate to the lives around you despite your current state of mind. Through the actual prayers, affirmations and scriptural references in this book you will gain insight on how to develop a new perspective on all aspects of your life and the situations that govern them.

This new perspective will then change how you process the world around you and in turn will change your words your actions, your habits, your character and your destiny. He continues to enjoy teaching his audiences on the many advantages of a holistic approach to the care of one's mind, body and soul.

With a personal commitment to empower women and the lives they touch; Sean's newest books are written specifically for women. "Bruised Yet Priceless" and it's Spanish version "Lastimada Pero Invaluable" is a companion guide for women on overcoming betrayal, deep hurt and resentment. Single and Complete is also a guide for the single woman on how to become personally fulfilled intellectually, spiritually and emotionally through the fulfillment in The Man Christ Jesus before seeking it in any man. This book will also be available in Spanish very soon.

With a waiting list of manuscripts from promising authors, Sean hopes to dispel the myths and barriers that prevent storytellers and authors from sharing their thoughts. His newly launched True Perspective Publishing House mission is "to thoroughly empower each of our authors with proficiency and access to tell their story without boundaries.

Sean's Vision Statement as a Speaker, Perspective Coach and Publisher is "***There is a chord of commonality that*** *is interwoven within every being within the human family. Although ideologies and geographical locale may separate us; it is the hope of True Perspective Publishing that our books and authors may identify that chord, which is the Spirit of God more readily to the eye and heart of mankind.*

Sean also authors Snack Food for the Soul, a weekly newsletter that inspires and challenges the thought process of its thousands of readers worldwide. Sean Blogs for Psychology Today.com, serves on the American Cancer Society's Operations Committee, serves on the advisory board and writes for Healthy Living Magazine and is a Mental Health Examiner for The Orlando Examiner.

 Sean received his bachelor's and master's degree in theological Studies from Vision, University in Ramona, California. Sean is married to Deborah and has three children; Chanel, Christian and Aaron

www.ingramcontent.com/pod-product-compliance
Lightning Source LLC
Chambersburg PA
CBHW030933090426
42737CB00007B/406